the
INTIMACY
COVER-UP

the
INTIMACY
COVER-UP

uncovering the difference
between love and sex

P. Roger hillerstrom
karlyn hillerstrom

Kregel
Publications

To Beth
my friend, my teammate, my wife.
After twenty-five years, we're still realizing that
genuine intimacy is a lot more work than
writing a book. Thanks.

—*Roger*

To my future husband.
I look forward to you with all of my heart.
Sharing life with you is going to be awesome!
I love you.

—*Karlyn*

contents

A Word of Thanks from Roger 9

A Word of Thanks from Karlyn 11

Introduction 13

1. Uncovering the Trap 15
   Karlyn's Thoughts: Balancing Act?

2. The Search for Intimacy 26
   Karlyn's Thought's: I Am Weak ... But He Is Strong

3. Cohabitation Confusion 40
   Karlyn's Thoughts: I Love You ... I Think

4. The Illicit Effect 54
   Karlyn's Thoughts: What You Know Will Hurt You

5. The Technical Virginity Trap 66
   Karlyn's Thoughts: Standard Decision

6. Sexual Addiction 84
   Karlyn's Thoughts: Overwhelming Infection

7. The Other Side of the Coin 102
        Karlyn's Thoughts: Slow and Steady Wins the Race

8. Discovering Freedom 114
        Karlyn's Thoughts: Then One Thing Led to Another

9. A Very, Very Old Message 129
        Karlyn's Thoughts: Receiving the Real Treasure

    Afterword 144
    Appendix: "Hello, Doctor . . . ?" 148
    Endnotes 173

A word of thanks from Roger

Any book is the work of many people beyond the author, who happens to get all the credit. I'm indebted to many people who have added their insight, wisdom, and life to this work.

To my wife, Beth, whose unique insights, life experience, and wisdom shape so much of what I think and do. Thanks, Sweetie. You're amazing!

To my dear friends, life-comrades, and fellow travelers who serve as my sounding board, frame of reference, and reality testers—Mark Robertson, Bill Henderson, Ron Rock, Bob Sturm, and Dan Garries. Keep in shape, guys; you'll be my pallbearers.

To my partners at Heritage Counseling Associates who've seen me through more than twenty years of personal and professional development—Dr. Grant Martin, Dr. Claude McCoy, Jackie McCoy, and Dr. Larry Bailey. Good friends and respected colleagues who've shaped me more than they know.

To Carrie Abbott, whose endless flow of encouragement and insight is a blessing that's contagious.

To Vicki Dihle, whose hard work and expertise did what I could not.

9

To Dennis Hillman and the editors at Kregel Publications, who had the confidence in this book to risk pushing it through to print.

To my friend Barry Landis who, through trial and error, is working with me and my role of Hyper-Turbo Dad. Hang in there, Barry, it's well worth it.

A word of thanks
from Karlyn

To the Man who is my strength, my comfort, my laughter, my encouragement, my friend, and my love through everything: Jesus. I would *be* nothing, I would *know* nothing, and I would *impact* nothing without You. I love You more every day.

To Mom and Dad. As the firstborn I've been "privileged" to be your guinea pig. The things you've taught me have shaped me as a person, and despite our periodic frustrations, I'm grateful that God put me in your family! As I grow up and make my own place in the world, I proudly carry with me your fingerprints on my life.

To my incredible boyfriend, Barry. Thanks for not running the other way when you found out what you were really getting into! I've been blessed by your wisdom, your outlook on life, and your excitement for ministry. Life with you is always an adventure, and I've never been on a greater one. Even in the hard times . . . falling is so much fun!

To my best friend, Mary Frances. You are my source for rationality, my partner in crime, my sounding board. Your friendship has a huge part in making me who I am. Till we're hilarious old ladies with no teeth and eyebrow rings, you'll be my better half.

To Dana, my close friend and mentor. You have reshaped me forever. I've been so blessed to watch from the inside as you live through struggles with joy and transparency, and taint everything in life with your own "special" brand of humor. You've taught me much about "the other side of life."

To Randy, who's been my "brother" for many years; you've changed me forever. I'm constantly learning from your unwavering friendship and hard-core passion for Jesus.

To my friend Brendan, with whom I first began discovering the complicated workings of a relationship. Our friendship has blessed and taught me so much, Bren—thank you.

To Jen and Kathleen, who spent many years investing themselves in me and my class at NBC—to describe what you've done for me would take more than a book. I'm grateful.

To amazing friends, especially my senior class at NBC: I wish I could list you all. The pieces of yourselves that you've put in my life will always be there. You've taught me much—I love you all!

introduction

The first book I wrote on this topic, *Intimate Deception,* was published in 1989. At that time very little had been written about the effect of premarital sex on the development of marriage and intimate relationships. The painful patterns were played out in my office daily, but the alternatives to therapy were few. *Intimate Deception* was well received; I continue to get calls, notes, and clients as a result of people reading that book.

Fifteen years have passed. My hair has a bit more gray, and my face has a few more wrinkles. I've published two other books—*Your Family Voyage* and *Adult to Adult*—and, with my partners, started a counseling clinic. In that time the principles of *Intimate Deception* haven't changed a bit. Though the principles are unchanged, it's time for the material to be updated with current research and statistics. There are also additional issues that now need to be addressed. So, I decided to rewrite the book.

During those fifteen years, my firstborn daughter has grown up. She has a voice of her own, with insights and life experiences to complement this old guy's perspective. It's been a delight to have her as a coauthor, adding her own spin to these truths. While my writing reflects twenty years of clinical practice and walking with people in pain, Karlyn brings the freshness, innocence, and hopefulness of a young heart. Her writing is a reflection of this particular stage of her life. Just as God has sculpted my thinking over the years, I look forward to watching His loving hand shape Karlyn. Age changes perspective, and for many readers her words today will resonate in ways mine cannot.

Though I've tried to keep this book from being offensively explicit, this is not a book for children. I've written to adults who want to improve their relationships. For those who are unmarried, its purpose is to help them develop healthy relationships in which emotional intimacy can grow and flourish. For married couples, its goal is to restore and rebuild relationships that have been damaged by poor decisions regarding sexuality. For parents, pastors, and youth leaders, it is a tool for dealing with the questions, concerns, and fears of young people in a society that has profoundly confused the purpose of sexual relationships.

As you read this book, my prayer is that you will find what you need to strengthen, deepen, and perhaps heal your closest relationships.

—P. ROGER HILLERSTROM

I

uncovering the trap

You're the one who's crazy!" Susan was angry and offended. "Just because I happen to enjoy being intimate doesn't mean my psyche is messed up. I think *you're* the one who needs a shrink! Sex is nothing more than two caring people touching each other; as long as both people enjoy it and no one gets hurt, there's nothing wrong with it. It's beautiful and clean and good. It's people like *you* who make sex dirty!"

Susan's father had brought his attractive, nineteen-year-old daughter into my office for psychological evaluation. His concern stemmed from her sexual promiscuity. He leaned back in his chair, staring intensely at his daughter. "This whole conversation is disgusting! Decent people don't even talk about such things. When I was your age I had never even imagined the things you're doing. No one had heard of herpes or AIDS. Men and women could fall in love without behaving like animals." His voice trailed off to almost a whisper. "The world was a better place then."

Susan and her father illustrate the vast differences in sexual attitudes held by our culture. Parents and their children sometimes disagree so drastically in their views that there's no apparent room for understanding, let alone compromise. Even within the same generation we see huge differences in values, opinions, and practices. The very nature and function of the sexual relationship seems unclear at times. The result for countless individuals is confusion and estrangement from healthy relationships.

so, what's new?

This conflict and confusion may seem like a product of the "now" generation, but that's far from the truth. The turmoil has been going on for centuries. Civilization goes through shifts in its sexual attitudes and approaches to sexuality, and history shows the swing in the pendulum of sexual values.

The prim Victorian era of the late nineteenth century reflected one extreme. The fear of sensuality and sinful behavior ran so high that it brought about a custom of sewing covers for table legs. It was thought that the sight of a leg, even a table leg, might stimulate lustful thoughts.

That era gave way to the Roaring Twenties, a period of economic as well as moral indulgence. Women raised their skirts, cut their hair, and smoked cigarettes. Talking about sex and writing books about sex were no longer taboo. Sexual freedom was in.

The thirties brought the Great Depression, and with it a resurgence of conservative values. Sexual attitudes became less and less a topic of conversation. "Taboo" was back in style.

It wasn't until the Baby Boom of the late forties and early fifties that the pendulum began to swing in the other direction. The war was over, the economy was looking better, and the Kinsey Report brought sex back into the spotlight.

During the sixties and seventies, rock 'n' roll, hippies, and the playboy philosophy enjoyed their heyday. *Grass, acid,* and *free love* were common terms along with *burned out, overdose,* and *VD.*

Each time the pendulum swings, it swings a little further and stays there a little longer. With each extreme, individuals as well as society experience negative consequences.

The good old days

I've talked to many people of all ages who grew up in an era or a home environment that presented sex as inherently evil. Perceived by some women of many generations as an unpleasant experience required of wives for their husbands, sexual intercourse has been considered by some religious groups to be an act distasteful to God but necessary for procreation. And some Christians even assume that sex must be the result of the fall of Adam and Eve, therefore making it something to be strictly controlled by God through multiple regulations, commandments, and penalties. The influence of that perspective is still strong in many families today.

The results are predictable. Fears and anxieties about sexual behavior are common. People are uncomfortable discussing problems involved in sexual relationships. Guilt and confusion about sex is probably the most common experience of all.

Fear, anxiety, guilt, and *confusion* are terms that describe the sexual atmosphere of previous generations, and to some degree, segments of this generation. But the pendulum continues to swing.

The new "solution"?

The current swing of the sexual pendulum seems to reflect and encourage a perspective opposite that of previous generations. Television shows promote sex, commercials advertise it, Hollywood glamorizes it, parents tolerate it, and churches ignore it. *U.S. News and World Report* presents a picture for us:

> "Have you ever heard a sermon on 'living together'?" asks religious columnist Michael McManus in his 1995 book, *Marriage Savers.* Condemnation of adult premarital sex has virtually vanished from religious preaching, even in the homilies of Catholic Priests. "In the pulpits there has been a backing away from moralizing about sex before marriage," says Bishop James McHugh, the bishop of Camden, N.J.

Why such reticence? The answer may seem obvious. Americans, at least tacitly, have all but given up the notion that the appropriate premarital state is one of chastity. The Bible may have warned that, like the denizens of Sodom and Gomorrah, those who "give themselves over to fornication" will suffer the "vengeance of eternal fire." Yet for most Americans, adult premarital sex has become the "sin" they not only wink at but quietly endorse. On television, adult virgins are about as rare as caribou in Manhattan. Several studies have found that prime-time network shows implicitly condone premarital sex, and air as many as 8 depictions of it for every 1 of sex between married couples.

Yet this surface consensus reflects a rather rapid—and surprisingly complex—transformation in American attitudes. The notion that sex ought to be reserved for marriage may now seem antiquated, but it wasn't very long ago that a large majority of Americans held just that belief. As late as 1968, for example, millions of Americans found it newsworthy that two unwed twenty-year-old college students would publicly admit to living together. Newspapers and newsmagazines replayed the tale of Linda LeClair, a sophomore at Barnard College, and Peter Behr, a Colombia University undergraduate, who conceded they had violated Barnard College's housing regulations by "shacking up" together in an off-campus apartment.

TV's characterization of out-of-wedlock sex has also done a flip-flop. Sen. Daniel Patrick Moynihan might say that television's treatment of premarital sex is a classic example of "defining deviancy down"—what was once considered deviant or abnormal now is treated as the norm. In his book *Prime Time*, Robert Lichter and his colleagues at the center for Media and Public Affairs found that prime-time television now by implication endorses unmarried adults' intention to have sex in about three out of four cases and raises concerns only about 5 percent of the time. "On shows like *Three's Company*, the characters hinted around a lot about premarital sex," says

Lichter. "But the shows back then did not specifically seek to justify unmarried sex." Producers and screenwriters appear largely inured to this permissiveness, though viewers seem troubled. In a *U.S. News* poll last year, just 38 percent of the Hollywood elite were concerned about how TV depicted premarital sex, compared with 83 percent of the public. "Hollywood has glorified adult premarital sex," argues Sen. Joseph Lieberman. "And that is unhelpful if your goal is to reduce teen pregnancy and out-of-wedlock births."

In this climate, the suggestion that abstinence is preferable to sex for unwed adults seems hopelessly retrograde, about as timely as recommending that hansom cabs replace automobiles. It is virginity that now makes news.[1]

The pressure to engage in sexual activity is no surprise. Our society reinforces the message at every turn. Study after study reflects the influence of the popular media—television, movies, videos, and music—in driving this trend toward promiscuous sexuality. One survey has shown that in the course of a year the average viewer sees on primetime TV more than 9,000 scenes that suggest sexual intercourse or present sexual innuendo. Young people are bombarded with the message that premarital sexual activity is normal, desirable, and mature. They are taught, in fact, that to be popular and sophisticated they need to be sexually active.

The results of this cultural bias are predictable. In this morally re-laxed atmosphere, sex becomes separated from commitment so that premarital sex appears normal and healthy. Sexually transmitted diseases (STDs) such as syphilis, gonorrhea, genital herpes, and AIDS exist in alarming numbers at every level of society. Our society is plagued by unwanted pregnancy, illegitimate children, and unwed teenage mothers. A crisis has emerged over the topic of abortion, which too often is the desire to destroy the children produced as a result of sexual irresponsibility.

Every year three million teenagers acquire an STD, many of which are incurable.[2] Fifteen percent of sexually active teenage girls have been found to be infected with the human papilloma virus, many with a strain of the virus linked to cervical cancer.[3] The Centers for Disease Control (CDC) estimates that between 100,000 and 150,000 women become infertile every year due to STD-related pelvic infection. Between 1983 and 1993 the number of unmarried mothers increased by 60 percent. In 1999, one study found that almost one million teenage girls—10 percent of all fifteen- to nineteen-year-old females—were becoming pregnant each year.[4] In 1996, about 274,000 abortions were performed on teenagers.[5] According to Guttmacher Institute studies, 40 percent of ninth graders and more than half of seventeen-year-olds say they have already had sex.[6]

While the statistics are alarming, the consequences plunge even deeper. Many of the results of these sexual attitudes are not so obvious. As a family therapist, I regularly see the effects of our society's attitude toward premarital sex—usually years later and most often in marriages. Lack of intimacy, lack of trust, communication problems, sexual dysfunction . . . the list goes on and on. These all stem from an act our society promotes as healthy and desirable. But we are just now beginning to see a new soberness toward sexual promiscuity. In light of disease epidemics and spiritual, emotional, and relational emptiness, many people are ready for the pendulum to swing in the other direction.

where do we go from here?

Both viewpoints—sexual laxity and sexual rigidity—are distortions of the truth. They are overreactions based on ignorance and result in serious and unnecessary consequences. Neither viewpoint is an accurate reflection of a healthy sexual relationship, nor a reasonable understanding of how sexual relationships function.

Imagine that you've just purchased your dream car, a brand-new Corvette. This is an incredible machine. Two million horsepower, zero to ninety in one-half second. There's not a scratch on it; it's beautiful! Every part of this engine is finely honed to perfection and precisely tuned. Everything is just as it should be. It's capable of absolute top performance. You bring this vehicle home and fill the gas tank with water.

Now, what if you really believe that the car will not be affected by water in the tank? What if you've decided not to let water make a difference in the car's performance? It doesn't matter what you've decided is true or what you hope for. The car won't run. Period. Your belief isn't a variable. The car wasn't designed to function this way, and all the rationalizing in the world won't change that. Your investment in this car should lead you to study it, because it's worth the effort to understand how it functions best.

We invest a great deal of ourselves in our closest relationships. It's well worth our time and energy to understand what will make these relationships work well. In this book we explore a significant aspect of these relationships to help you make them function to their utmost capacity and satisfaction.

Today many young couples are asking important questions about their sexual relationships:

"Why not practice our sexual response to each other just like we practice other things before marriage, such as communication and decision making?"

"Since we're committed to each other, why wait for a piece of paper?"

"We love each other and we'll get married. Isn't that what really matters?"

"Isn't it rigid and legalistic to adhere to a set of ethics from a totally different culture and context than our own?"

"Isn't God more interested in love and relationship than in a marriage license?"

These questions deserve responses, and they, as well as many others, will be answered in the following chapters.

This is a book about the deception and confusion involved in misunderstanding natural and healthy sexual functioning. By correcting these misunderstandings and changing our approach to intimate relationships, we as individuals, and perhaps as a society, can avoid the destruction and pain that is so common today.

In these chapters we explore "this confusion" from the fields of psychology, sociology, and medicine. We examine its impact on relationships as well as on individual emotional and sexual development. Finally, we explore ways of avoiding these traps or, if already caught, how to climb out of them.

At the end of each chapter I've provided a section titled "Growing Closer." The purpose of this section is to help the reader recognize, evaluate, and avoid potential traps associated with intimate relationships, as well as to provide guidelines for developing genuine intimacy through communication.

Growing closer

1	2	3	4	5	6	7	8	9	10

Conservative   **Liberal**

1. Place an *X* above the number that represents where you think you are on a continuum between extremely liberal and extremely conservative in sexual attitudes.
2. Place an *A* above the number where you think most people in your age group are.
3. Are your feelings about the placement of your *X* more positive than negative, or vice versa?
4. How do you think your view of your peers affects where you placed yourself on the continuum?
5. What was the attitude toward sex in your parents' families?
6. How did that attitude influence the atmosphere in the home in which you grew up?
7. If you are married, how does that attitude influence your marriage and family life today?

Karlyn's Thoughts
Balancing Act?

I've seen all three Austin Powers movies.

That's a fact I'm not proud of. I hate Austin Powers. During all three movies, I sat there, telling myself, "This is ridiculous. This is gross. You don't need to be watching this!" But I did anyhow. Why? It was funny. It was entertaining. And my friends were laughing.

When I watched the third one, *Goldmember,* it was with a roomful of guys—Christian guys—who, when a suggestive commercial came on TV, would all look in another direction and pointedly ignore the nearly naked women prancing around on the screen. Their determination to be pure was something I admired about them, so I didn't understand why they thought this movie was so hilarious. In my mind it was worse than any Victoria's Secret commercial: it was two hours long, for one thing, and it had everything the commercials had and more. There was a plethora of breasts nearly bursting out of tiny shirts, barely covered rear ends shaking it in front of the camera, casual sex glorified all over the place, and absolutely disgusting sexual innuendoes and jokes saturating the entire movie. Forty years ago this PG-13 film would've never made it out of the perverted, lust-crazed mind that created it! Why is it so entertaining today, even for Christians who are striving to be clean-minded? There's a fine line that lies between being a prude and being pure, and a finer line between being pure and being tolerant. Could it be that in our well-intentioned attempts to reach the world, we've crossed that finer line without noticing it?

In physics, an object being pulled in two different directions by equally strong forces will stay right where it is. As a Christian, you've got the world pulling you from one side and God pulling you from another. You have to decide what you're going to do with those two forces. If you try to adopt pieces of both, you'll become stuck in the middle—unable to pick one way or the other and unwilling to surrender to anyone's total control.

In my short twenty years on earth, I've learned that life is one big balancing act. Over and over I have to learn how to balance one extreme against the other in order to find a workable solution. I mean seriously, we've been taught from childhood that balance is important: the kid who couldn't learn to compromise went home with report cards saying, "Doesn't play well with others!" Well, I've got a new suggestion for you—one that probably wouldn't make me very popular with elementary schoolteachers. Maybe learning balance in life doesn't necessarily mean to compromise evenly and fairly. It doesn't mean taking what God says and mixing it into our culture so that we come out with a solution that makes us look reasonable, that works in our social circles with the least disruption possible, and that doesn't make us look like screaming fanatics. Sometimes we *are* the screaming fanatics, even if we're not really screaming!

Instead, God deliberately chose things the world considers foolish in order to shame those who think they are wise. And he chose those who are powerless to shame those who are powerful. God chose things despised by the world, things counted as nothing at all, and used them to bring to nothing what the world considers important, so that no one can ever boast in the presence of God. (1 Corinthians 1:27–29 NLT)

You could look stupid if you refused to watch a socially acceptable film like Austin Powers. People will probably think you're some kind of repressed freak. Your friends might tease you for being uptight. But guess what? That's what happens when you bring the undiluted commands of Jesus into a sinful world. It hurts because it's supposed to: "The world would love you if you belonged to it, but you don't. I chose you to come out of the world, and so it hates you" (John 15:19 NLT). When a decision hurts, that probably means it was the right one. You know the pain you get after you've worked out really hard, those aching muscles that scream when you wake up the next day to let you know you made a difference? We like to call that a "good kind of hurt." The pain you receive from exercising God's law is a "good kind of hurt," too. If nothing hurts once in a while . . . nothing's changing. You're not getting stronger. You've got to step out and *let* it hurt sometimes in order to grow in your understanding and love of God.

Balancing life isn't about finding a happy medium between God's commands and our comfort; it's about constantly learning to die to self and to let Him take over. As one—desire for self—decreases, the other—Jesus' power in us—increases. Surrender is the only way to find momentum for your life. Spending your life trying not to rock anyone's boat is only going to get you stuck between two worlds.

So what's it going to be? Stuck or surrendered? In this book we'll talk about what it looks like to use God's point of view on relationships in a world that doesn't care about God's point of view. It's going to hurt. You're not going to like everything you find out about yourself. But I promise you that you'll be changed.

Decide to stop the balancing act. Decide to take His hand and let Him lead you in this adventure of challenging the power of our culture.

ב

The search for intimacy

Nate and Carol wanted to explore their relationship in preparation for marriage. They'd been dating for almost two years when they came to me, and they got along wonderfully. They'd spent a great deal of time with one another and had shared a broad range of experiences.

Nate and Carol were deeply in love and enjoyed everything they did together. While neither expressed any specific concerns in their relationship, both agreed that some things probably needed work. They wanted their future marriage to be a healthy one, so premarital counseling seemed like a logical move.

Within three months of our first meeting, it was clear that there were things worth working on. Over the course of our five sessions together things had changed between them. They began to feel angry and frustrated with each other, and both expressed a great deal of hurt in the relationship. These feelings were new for them, but because of a discussion we'd had in our very first session together, they were no surprise to me. In that first session we talked about their sexual relationship, which had been initiated shortly after they began to date. After I shared some of my concerns regarding premarital sexual relationships, they agreed to refrain from sex and remain celibate during the course of our sessions.

In our early sessions, Nate and Carol enjoyed comparing temperament scales and discussing their family histories together. When, to-gether, they planned a hypothetical budget and baby-sat children, however, they began to feel less comfortable. Before long, the home-work discussions began to focus on emotional issues and the process became downright difficult.

This growing tension was a surprise to them. Theirs had not been a standard dating relationship of dinner and movies on weekends. These two had done all sorts of things together. They'd shopped together, cooked meals together, traveled together. They'd spent time with one another's families and friends. This was not a union of two strangers, but somehow it was beginning to feel that way to them.

A number of the conflicts that arose seemed trivial, but the emo-tional load they carried was significant. At one point Carol expressed what they both were feeling: "I've never seen this side of you. It's like I hardly know you. I'm not so sure about this whole thing anymore." It was obvious that this "intimate" couple had not been as intimate as they'd thought.

sex and intimacy

The need for emotional closeness and intimacy is inherent in hu-man nature. We all want to be loved for who we are, not just for what we can do or give to someone. The sexual bond functions as an ex-pression of that intimacy, but it can never be the source of it. This is a distinction that many people fail to make.

In our society we've been taught to label sex as "intimate." The words *sex* and *intimacy* are, in fact, often used interchangeably. This reflects a gross misunderstanding of the true nature of intimacy. It also propa-gates a myth about the role of sex in relationships.

Webster's Dictionary defines *intimacy* as "a familiarity characteriz-ing one's deepest nature, a close association marked by warm friend-ship developing through long association." Intimacy is knowing and being known—deeply. It involves building trust, along with sharing experiences and personal information. That takes time and effort—lots of it.

A couple's sexual relationship prior to marriage can easily create what I call "artificial intimacy." Artificial intimacy describes the *sensation* of closeness that is inherent in mutual sexual arousal. Our bodies feel good being close to one another. Often we equate that good feeling with trust and openness. Yet that sensation is deceptive because it can *feel* vulnerable, emotionally open, and trusting when it's not at all. Think about that for a moment. Sexual intercourse can occur without any trust, emotional vulnerability, or shared history. Two people can have sex without knowing each other's names. If sex were truly and necessarily intimate, prostitution couldn't exist. Yet it's physically possible to have a sexual relationship with a complete stranger and still have that false sense of intimacy. A couple may feel close when they're not close at all. Their intimacy is artificial—not real.

The All-purpose problem solver?

Sex can even be used to *avoid* intimacy. Couples do it all the time, most of them without knowing it. Here's how it works. When emotional needs are not being met or when some problem exists, tension and conflict thrive. The tension may result from a disagreement or from a difference in perspective, values, or mood. He, for example, may live from paycheck to paycheck, while she, from an early age, learned to save and budget . Or she may want to spend what he thinks is an inordinate amount of time with her parents, which doesn't make sense to him; after all, he was on his own from the age of sixteen. Whatever the source of the conflict, it almost always means that something needs to be talked out. Conflict can be a sign of life and health in a relationship, but when conflict isn't resolved, it becomes a barrier to closeness. When conflict is ignored, hidden, or denied, the relationship is in danger.

Sexually active couples often use the sensation of intimacy to deny the existence of conflict. A couple can go to bed, feel great about each other, and never resolve the real issue. Problems don't get resolved, they just get buried under artificial intimacy.

This pattern can continue for a long time. The source of conflict often remains hidden, in fact, until unresolved tension develops into resentment. Frequently, the woman feels resentment first. As resentment builds, sexual intercourse no longer feels intimate because the emotional barriers are so high. This usually happens after a couple has been married for a while. Then the response is usually one of hopelessness. He or she may say things like, "All the love has gone out of our marriage; there's nothing left." The issue isn't that something has gone out of the relationship but that something was built into it—a pattern of escape and denial based upon sexual feelings of arousal instead of upon healthy communication.

The Depths of Intimacy

Let's take *Webster's* definition of *intimacy* to a more practical level. Genuine intimacy is a relationship of mutual, honest self-disclosure and acceptance. This definition may give us a clearer picture of what intimacy looks like.

In an intimate relationship, I'm willing to share information about myself that could be used to hurt me. I experience acceptance from the other person, in spite of my vulnerability, and I give that acceptance as well.

We can think of intimacy in terms of five levels, or depths, of vulnerability. These levels can be recognized by the topics of conversation that I'm willing to share. At each level I become more open to rejection and emotional pain in the relationship.

Level 1: Superficial "Reports"

"Sure is a nice day."
"The Lakers won last night."
"That sunset sure is gorgeous."
These statements are examples of superficial interaction. There's nothing inherently wrong with them, but they tell you almost nothing about the speaker. When a relationship consists primarily of this level of vulnerability, we wouldn't consider it as being deep.

Level 2: Third-Party Perspectives and Beliefs

"Yesterday the president said . . ."
"My pastor believes . . ."
"My uncle always used to say . . ."
In these statements, I'm choosing a source to quote and, therefore, beginning to share part of myself by association. I am not, however, directly sharing anything about myself, and so I can be safe from criticism or rejection. After all, I didn't say it, my pastor did. Level 2 involves more vulnerability than level 1, but not much.

Level 3: My Own Perceptions and Beliefs

"I think every Christian should serve in the military."
"I don't think a parent should ever spank a child."
"I think it's wrong to be in debt."
Now I'm telling you what I think about things. Here I begin to share directly a part of myself. I'm giving you intellectual input. If I sense your rejection or I feel too vulnerable, I can switch my opinion and get safe. I can still avoid conflict and emotional pain fairly easily at this level simply by changing my mind, or at least telling you I've that changed it.

Level 4: My Personal History

"My greatest accomplishment was a bike ride across the state."
"Every girlfriend I've had has dumped me."
"When I was sixteen, I had an abortion."
Now I'm starting to share intimately. I'm telling you about things I've done and choices I've made, experiences I'm proud of and ashamed of. When I share my history with you, I'm getting vulnerable because I can't change my past. If you're going to reject me on the basis of my background, I can't retract it or pretend it's not so. If you reject me here, my only safety will be in convincing you or myself that my past doesn't affect me today.

Level 5: My Feelings and Emotional Reactions

"I'm hurt by what you said."

"I'm angry about what happened."

"I feel important and close to you."

This level of vulnerability is where genuine intimacy lies. My emotional reactions don't change quickly. So if I'm hurt by something today, I'll probably be hurt by it tomorrow. If I entrust you with my feelings and you reject me on that basis, I have no option for escape as in steps 1–4. I must simply feel the pain. It's also true that when I share vulnerable feelings with you, you have the option to use them against me later. That will be even more painful than sharing them initially. Thus, I'm trusting you with something precious and fragile.

For many, the concept of levels of vulnerability is a tough one to grasp. Especially for men who, at least in our culture, haven't been taught to pay much attention to emotions. Think of it this way. Let's say you and I are sitting comfortably, having a pleasant conversation. As we're talking I say to you, "I think you're one of the smartest people I know." Think for a moment about the feeling that generates inside you right now. It's probably a good feeling. Maybe you feel pride, confidence, or gratitude. Maybe you feel close to me at that moment. In terms of our levels of intimacy, I'm sharing at a level 3— a little vulnerable, not too deep, but it's a good feeling for both of us. Now let me add a level 5 feeling statement, and you pay attention to how your own feeling is affected. "I think you're one of the smartest people I know, and I feel embarrassed to be around you." Notice any change inside you? Chances are, you don't feel quite the same as you did before I shared my feelings. Let's try another one. "I think you're one of the smartest people I know, and I feel humbled that you like me." Any change in your own feeling here? How about this one? "I think you're one of the smartest people I know, and I'm proud to know you."

In each case, your own feelings are impacted as I share mine. How you react to me will be a result of your own emotions. Since I don't have control over your emotional response, I may feel anxious about sharing at this level. If I avoid that anxiety by not sharing my emotions, our relationship doesn't deepen.

Keeping these patterns in mind, let's get back to Nate and Carol. From our first session I noticed a very common pattern in their communication. In a discussion, Carol would freely talk about her feelings and reactions to situations, often relating these to her childhood (levels 4 and 5). Nate would respond in these discussions by referring to books he'd read or things he'd heard (level 2). Seldom, if ever, did he share his personal, emotional responses with her.

Neither of them could see this imbalance in their relationship. It was clear that Carol was far more emotionally invested in the relationship and was sharing more deeply and vulnerably. Nate was keeping an emotional distance by risking very little of himself. Because they "felt" intimate, both were oblivious to the dangerous emotional chasm between them.

To help Nate and Carol understand the concept of artificial intimacy, I shared the following illustration. A couple's relationship before marriage can be compared to a steam pipe that contains and transports pressure. The pipe has several small cracks that are invisible to the eye. At the end of the pipe is an exhaust valve that can be opened or closed. As long as the valve is open, the pressure is released and the cracks never emit any steam—they're never discovered and repaired. Eventually they'll corrode and destroy the pipe. Only when the valve remains closed so that pressure can build can the cracks be discovered and repaired.

All couples have weak points—or cracks—in their communication patterns: different viewpoints, biases, sensitivities, family differences, role expectations. Since communication is the area of real intimacy, these cracks are important to discover. But if a couple is opening the exhaust valve of sex, normal pressure doesn't have the chance to build. Many communication flaws won't become evident until they are severe. And for many couples, that's too late.

What Nate and Carol came to understand is this: by continuing their sexual relationship, they were keeping the valve open. As long as they were releasing pressure that way, they couldn't accomplish their premarital objectives. They needed to close the valve to evaluate realistically their patterns of communication. As they stopped sexually releasing emotional pressure, they began to experience irritations and reactions that hadn't been evident. The cracks emitted some steam, and they began to discover what to work on in their relationship in preparation for marriage.

Nate and Carol found a powerful side benefit. Since they had to find new ways of dealing with their sexual feelings, they learned to be creative in expressing affection. Written notes, small but significant gifts, shared secrets, shared feelings (both positive and negative) in serious conversation, all became new ways of expressing affection toward one another. Nate and Carol learned many lessons in the art of romance that would pay rich dividends in their future marriage.

If they had kept the sexual valve open, premarital counseling would have been a waste of time and money, and they would have set themselves up for potential marriage problems later on. Fortunately, Nate and Carol understood the seriousness of their situation and were willing to do whatever it took to prepare for marriage. Some of the steps I suggested to them will be discussed in a later chapter on setting standards in dating and courtship.

Growing closer

1. What is your definition of intimacy? Is it different from the definition in this chapter?
2. Is there something about you—a fear, a failure, or some deep hurt from your past—that you're unwilling to share with someone else? Write down the characteristics of a relationship in which you would feel safe sharing this fact with another person. Be as specific as you can. What does this list of characteristics tell you about your concept of intimacy?
3. Think of the person you would call your closest friend, or if you are married, think of your spouse. Would you say that you are emotionally intimate with him or her? What behaviors are you using to define intimacy in this relationship?

4. Think of a friend with whom you are not emotionally intimate. What are the differences between that relationship and
   the one mentioned in question 2?

For Those Who Are Married

First, as individuals and without sharing your answers with your
partner, write down your responses to the following statements as
honestly and completely as you can.

1. Circle your opinion in the appropriate column:

1	2	3	4	5
strongly disagree	mildly disagree	undecided	mildly agree	strongly agree

Husband   **Wife**

1 2 3 4 5   Our relationship is as emotionally   1 2 3 4 5
              intimate as I would like it to be.

1 2 3 4 5   I openly share my thoughts and   1 2 3 4 5
              feelings without reservation.

1 2 3 4 5   My spouse openly shares thoughts   1 2 3 4 5
              and feelings without reservation.

1 2 3 4 5   During courtship we were more   1 2 3 4 5
              emotionally intimate than we are now.

2. Now go back and predict what you believe your spouse's responses will be. Use the other column for these answers.

3. Circle the appropriate response:

When I begin to feel emotionally vulnerable, my reaction is to . . .

- open up and share my fears
- become irritable and angry *(circled)*
- withdraw in silence *(circled)*
- crack a joke
- change the subject *(circled)*
- act as if it doesn't matter *(circled)*
- make sexual advances

4. From the above list, my partner's response to emotional vulnerability usually is _WITHDRAW or JOKE_ .
5. One thing I could do to deepen emotional intimacy in my marriage is _LISTEN MORE_ .
6. One thing I think my partner could do to deepen our emotional intimacy is _LISTEN & TALK_ .

Now, set aside an hour or two as a couple and discuss your individual responses.

Karlyn's Thoughts
I Am Weak . . . But He Is Strong

I'm normal.

All right, so most people who know me won't agree with that statement, but I can explain. I'm "normal" because I have emotional scars just like everyone else. I hide pieces of myself from others just like you do. I'm afraid of being rejected just as much as the next person.

Everyone carries the pain of being rejected at some point or another;

most of us have been rejected many times over. From the time we were in junior high, people have managed to find things about us that were distasteful, and we've learned to hide those things deep inside ourselves. After all, who enjoys being rejected? It's a normal human impulse to protect ourselves from pain. If you touch something hot, you automatically yank your hand away. If your heart gets crushed because someone didn't like a part of your character, you yank that part away from the public eye. It's the natural way to handle a "heart-hurt." Unfortunately, that reflex works against you.

Hurt over past rejection develops into a fear of future rejection. It results in the assumption that if someone sees you in a disagreeable moment, she or he will want nothing to do with you. I, for example, don't like people to know how much of a control freak I am, so I try to camouflage those feelings when they come up in group situations, and make them as deniable as possible. I've honestly worked on changing this part of my character, so I'm better than I used to be, but I'll never be a quiet follower. Sometimes the control freak in me just jumps out and snaps at some unsuspecting friend; when the moment passes, I'm left to blush in embarrassment as I apologize for this uglier side of my personality. For the next few weeks I'll be on my best behavior with that person, trying to convince him or her that what happened wasn't the *real* me.

I know you know what I'm talking about: we all have ugly parts of ourselves that we hide to avoid painful rejection. But we also know it's not possible to hide those parts forever, especially when we're around someone a lot. The more comfortable you get with a person, the more you'll let your guard down, and that means more of the real *you* is going to sneak out from time to time. When that happens and the person backs away from you, you're not surprised. You just retreat, lick your wounds, reprimand yourself for letting it slip again, and get on with life. But when people still accept you after the ugly piece has been exposed, that's a shocker. It'll take time before it sinks in that they really *won't* reject you. Gradually, you'll feel safe, and you'll want to reveal more of your real self to them. *That's* being intimate. Sharing the hidden parts of your heart is true intimacy.

I think it's fair to say that the majority of the undesirable pieces we keep hidden are our weaknesses. Who of us wants to show anyone else what makes us stumble? Weaknesses are *not* cool. Not only that, but revealing weaknesses makes us feel more vulnerable than to reveal parts of our character we don't like. To give you a personal example, I'll tell you that I struggle with lust. In my life, this is a weakness that can be set off by a movie scene, a suggestive joke on a night when I'm tired, or even a small compromise in physical boundaries with my boyfriend. I don't like letting people see how weak I am in this area. Especially because I'm a girl; girls are supposed to be the pure ones, right? When I was younger, before I found out that my close friends struggled with exactly the same thing, I really thought I was a bit of a freak. After all, lots of people have characteristics they don't like—like craving control—but it seems shameful for a girl to have a hard time keeping her thoughts pure or to struggle with masturbation or fantasies. And for guys, too; not being able to overcome something like lust can be embarrassing enough to become ashamed and want to go into hiding. Besides, the weakness of lust isn't something a person can just get rid of. I can't simply shake it off and get over it. Weaknesses are like bloodstains: they never come out completely.

How many people know your weaknesses? What does it take for you to be able to trust someone with the deepest, darkest, most secret parts of your heart? For all of us it certainly takes a lot of time and an intense level of trust. You risk everything when you let someone into your heart. Well, I'll let you in on a little secret: *that IS what it means to be truly intimate.* Do you want intimacy with your partner? It can't be found in arousing each other or being able to sexually excite one another. Anyone can be arousing! *True* intimacy is when you take off your external shell—the "you" that the whole world can see—and reveal the reality of the *you* underneath. It leaves you vulnerable. Opening yourself emotionally to another person takes incredible trust that she or he will accept what you're giving. The potential for heart-wrenching pain is off the charts, but without that risk, you'll never find the intimacy you seek.

On the other hand, there's an "intimacy" that can be created in less than an hour: the infomercial version—cheap, easy, and microwaveable, as seen on TV. No mess, no hassle, no refunds—it's called *false* intimacy. Sexual arousal will make you two feel so close. You might even be convinced that you've won this love game. But guess what? You just lost. Trying to create intimacy by using sex is like snatching the gold medal without running the race. You didn't earn it, it's not yours, and you'll pay for it eventually. You'd come out a lot better in the long run if you'd only gone through the hard work, poured out your own sweat and blood, and actually *earned* that medal. The real thing takes hard work, but every ounce of effort will be worth it. Keep this in mind: what you put into the relationship is what you'll get out of it.

Nobody goes into a romantic relationship hoping that it will end quickly. The whole point is to keep it alive! So why would you deliberately do things to sabotage the health of that relationship? The fact is, keeping a relationship healthy is hard work and not always fun, especially when it comes to staying physically pure. We don't always want to face the raw effort it takes to deny ourselves and do what *doesn't* feel good while we aim for an unseen goal. But *nothing worth having comes without a fight.* It's essential to understand the things that are deadly to a growing relationship and make sure they don't threaten yours. To keep your physical intimacy in check, here are some questions to honestly answer:

1. What are my partner's weaknesses?
2. How do my actions affect those weaknesses right now? How can I change my actions to affect those weaknesses differently?
3. What do I do to tempt my partner to give in to those weaknesses?
4. What can I do to help my partner avoid confrontations with those weaknesses?

How would your partner answer these questions about *you?* You're in this as a team, after all. This "protective love" is meant to flow both ways.

For these questions to do you any good, you've *got* to be willing to face the hard and uncomfortable choices with your significant other. It's not fun, I know—I don't always look forward to these kinds of conversations. Decisions that take away your immediate gratification are hard to follow up on. But if you want a relationship that strengthens you as a person as well as a couple, you must be determined to protect—not entice—your teammate. It's a struggle, but as a unified team, with God as your coach, you'll reach that unseen goal. Don't give up: the reward is greater than the risk.

3

cohabitation confusion

 Y ou were never this way before we were married!" Sandra's tearstained face was red with rage. "You lied to me for three years . . . the whole time we were living together."

"Look who's talking." Paul's restraint could not hide the emotional pain and anger just below the surface. "Any love you showed me ended on our wedding day. I should've never married you!"

A relationship that began with an earnest desire for mutual love and commitment had developed into a mockery of what the marriage bond could and should be. After three years of pleasant premarital living together, or cohabitation, and two years of tumultuous marriage, both Paul and Sandra were confused and hurt. Each felt deceived and betrayed by the other. Neither understood how such a thing could have happened.

Superficially, cohabitation seems logical. Few of us would buy a car without test-driving it first. Many of our major purchases, in fact, come with a money-back trial period. It seems to make sense to experiment and test a relationship before taking the life-changing step of marriage. Unfortunately, cohabitation, by its very nature, cannot serve that purpose. As a family therapist, I see almost daily the effect of cohabitation on marriages. Few individuals, however, understand the process whereby a seemingly rational approach to marriage preparation becomes a betrayal of the growing intimacy and trust of courtship.

Normal?

Statistically, Paul and Sandra fit the norm. In light of the "logic" of testing the marriage relationship, it seems strange that study after study reflects the devastating effects of cohabitation on relationships.

- Divorce rates for married couples who cohabited are consistently higher than for couples who didn't live together before the wedding.[1]
- One study of 3,300 couples found cohabiting couples to have a divorce rate 46 percent higher than noncohabitors.[2]
- A study by Yale and Columbia universities found divorce rates for cohabiting couples to be nearly 80 percent higher than for couples who do not cohabitate.[3]
- Cohabitation is associated with greater marital instability, lower marital satisfaction, and poorer communication in marriage.[4]
- Cohabiting couples report physical abuse three times more often than married couples.[5]
- Cohabiting women are four times more likely to be violently abused.[6]
- Cohabiting couples report higher levels of alcohol problems than among married people.[7]
- Depression rates among cohabiting couples are three times higher than those for married people.[8]
- Children in cohabiting households are more likely to have emotional or behavioral problems, do poorly academically, and live in poverty.[9]
- One study found that children of unmarried cohabiting biological parents are *twenty times* more likely to be abused than the children of married parents. When a mother lives with a boyfriend who is not the biological father, the children are *thirty-three times* more likely to be abused.[10]
- Another study concluded that "the evidence suggests that the most unsafe of all environments for children is that in which the mother is living with someone other than the child's biological father."[11]

Consider also that only 30 to 40 percent of couples who cohabit eventually marry and that most periods of cohabitation last under two years.[12] Since the majority of couples who live together decide not to marry, it would seem that the ones who do marry would have healthier, happier relationships. Study after study, though, indicates that just the opposite is true. Cohabitants who marry report more frequent disagreements, more fights, more violence, and lower levels of fairness in and happiness with their relationships compared to married couples who did not cohabit.[13] One study of over 13,000 adults showed that, compared to married couples who had not cohabited, couples who had cohabited before marriage reported greater marital conflict and poorer communication as well as a lower commitment to marriage. These couples had a significantly higher likelihood of divorce. Longer cohabitation was, in fact, associated with a higher likelihood of divorce.[14]

The statistical evidence is overwhelming—not a single statistic portrays cohabitation in a positive light. In spite of this, the number of couples who choose to live together before marriage increases each year. During the eighties, the number of unmarried couples living together in the United States soared by 80 percent to 2.9 million. And, according to the U.S. Census Bureau, between 1990 and 2000 the number of cohabiting couples increased by another 66 percent.[15] In a study of high school seniors, 60 percent agreed with this statement: "It is usually a good idea for a couple to live together before getting married in order to find out whether they really get along."[16] With so many negative indications regarding premarital living together, why is cohabitation becoming so popular and widely accepted in our culture? Because in regard to most relational principles, what our mainstream culture and the media present as "the norm" is 180 degrees from "healthy." In other words, our society has it backward.

Many people today aren't able to evaluate a relationship beyond the superficial. The common assumption seems to be that if two people enjoy being together, the relationship must be a good one. This simplistic approach leads to a great deal of hurt and confusion when relationships don't work out. Very little in our culture or in popular literature helps us understand the nature of genuine intimacy. In chapter 2, Nate and Carol were a typical example of this lack of understanding. Regardless of the reasons for this information void, all of us need to understand how healthy relationships function. This chapter illuminates and clarifies the confusion.

Remember, the key ingredient that differentiates living together from marriage is the "back door"—the option to leave without a lot of messy consequences. The logic goes something like this: "If things don't work out, we can chalk it up to experience and move on. At least we've learned something about ourselves and marriage." This sounds good in theory, but it doesn't work out that way in real life. The element of lifetime commitment is far more than a trivial detail; it affects every interaction, every expectation, and every response two individuals have to one another. To misunderstand this point is to lay the foundation for disaster in a relationship.

Double Messages

Communication is more than an exchange of words. We communicate on many levels, often without being aware of it. Our tone of voice can communicate a message more powerfully than the words we choose. We also communicate far more intensely and clearly with our behavior than we do verbally. It's been estimated that nonverbal messages are five times as powerful as the spoken word. This means that if my words say one thing and my behavior says another, you'll tend to believe my behavior even if you don't want to. The old saying "actions speak louder than words" is true.

When two opposite messages are communicated about the same situation at the same time, we call it a "double message." The classic double message is a parent saying to his or her teenager, "I want you to be independent, so do what I tell you," or, "I've told you a million times, never exaggerate."

Cohabiting couples communicate nonverbal, double messages every day. Paul and Sandra are a good example of this. They were in love and wanted to be together constantly. They felt as though they were ready for marriage, but each had been surprised and hurt in previous relationships that had broken up. Since both came from broken homes, they were strongly opposed to divorce. For them, the most logical solution seemed to be, "Let's live together in order to check it out." What could be more reasonable? So for three full years, they did just that.

By moving in together, Paul and Sandra were communicating a message to one another. That message was, "I desire intimacy with you. I want to get to know you deeply. I want to be one with you, and only living together will allow me to be that trusting and close to you." Picture them with arms open, coming toward each other.

But there's also a second message. It's conveyed by one or both of them not being willing to make the commitment of marriage. This message says, "Don't get too close. There's a limit. I don't want to get so close that I can't escape if you hurt me. I don't really trust you." The picture here is of Paul and Sandra, arms outstretched, backing away slowly.

Sandra and Paul may not have been consciously aware of the conflicting messages they were communicating to each other, but the messages came through loud and clear.

Dead End

The result of a double message in a relationship is a subtle but inherent lack of confidence. What is real and what is not real become confused. What is said and what is believed become two different things. Distrust and doubt are integrated at the very heart and core of the relationship.

After marriage, formerly cohabiting couples are surprised to discover how dissatisfied they've suddenly become. They feel an uneasiness that wasn't there before, and it's a confusing experience. What happened to this logical, well-planned relationship?

What happened is this: the wedding shut the "back door"—that option to leave the relationship if it becomes difficult or painful. Without this option, their comfortable relationship begins to close around them like a room with shrinking walls—exactly what they were trying to avoid. Suddenly their worst fears have come true. "What have I gotten myself into?" Since distrust and insecurity were built into the relationship long ago, the downhill slide to disaster isn't far away.

In a healthy marriage, commitment is at the heart of the relationship, regardless of the ebb and flow of emotions. For cohabiting couples who eventually marry, commitment is added on as a final touch.

More surprises

The theory of a trial marriage doesn't hold up for another reason. When a couple lives together without the commitment of marriage, the little irritations of daily living are no big deal:

- He doesn't empty the garbage, but so what? If you get tired of it, you can leave, right? No reason to make a fuss.
- She doesn't wash the dishes every day. No big deal. Since you're just testing this thing out, you focus on "real" problems. Besides, if you can just let it slide and go to bed, everything will be fine in the morning.

And so it goes for a hundred situations, most of which the individuals are not consciously aware.

Then it happens. The back door is closed with a marriage license. The impact of those little irritations changes. Now each one seems to be setting a lifetime precedent. The emotional response is, "It's going to be like this forever. It has to change, now." Those previously "unnoticed" little irritations are hair triggers for conflict, and it's a surprise to both partners since neither seemed to mind them before.

Habits and personal idiosyncrasies are the standard issues of marriages. To some degree all marriage partners must adjust and adapt, negotiate and compromise on issues like these. While the goal of cohabitation was to deal with these issues in advance, it seldom happens on any meaningful level.

The cohabiting couple who marries does so because they feel assured that they know one another well and that there will be few shocks awaiting them beyond the altar. When the couple begins to confront these irritations, the emotional impact can be devastating. In a healthy marriage the emotional response would be, "That bugs me." But in this situation the response is, "You lied to me." A normal marital irritation becomes an experience of betrayal. The partners feel deceived and trapped, often to the point of desperation.

These feelings of betrayal inevitably amplify the experience. Conflicts intensify quickly and often explosively. What once felt like trust now feels like entrapment. Partners become adversaries, cooperation becomes competition, vulnerability becomes self-protection.

What happened to the trial marriage? The fact is, there's no such thing. Trying to experience marriage without a lifetime commitment is like going to a doughnut shop to buy your meals. You can fill your stomach and convince yourself that you've taken nourishment, but eventually you'll die of malnutrition with your stomach full.

And furthermore . . .

Beyond these relational dynamics, several other important factors affect the cohabiting couple. Studies indicate that, compared to other couples, those who have cohabited prior to marriage have a number of characteristics not conducive to long-term relationships:

- Both men and women exhibit a lower commitment to marital fidelity. Before marriage, the incidence of infidelity was found to be twice as frequent for cohabitants, and after marriage, the incidence of adultery increased 39 percent for cohabiters.[17] Commitment and faithfulness are casualities of cohabitation.
- Although cohabitants have sex at least as often as married couples, they are less likely to say they enjoy it.[18] The "freedom" of cohabitation doesn't result in sexual fulfillment.
- A Harvard study found cohabiting couples to have lower levels of sexual satisfaction and sexual exclusivity as well as lower satisfaction with the marriage relationship in general. The study also found that cohabiting couples have more difficulties in

other relationships as well, especially with parents and family.[19] The support system so valuable in marriage tends to be weaker for couples who have cohabited.

- Cohabiting couples are found to have lower tolerance for unhappiness in a relationship and choose to leave a relationship rather than learn to work through differences.[20]

Two people living together easily rationalize, minimize, or deny these facts. Often the desire for the relationship distorts reality. When the relationship deteriorates, the couple is often unaware of how intimacy was sabotaged before it had a chance to develop. All in all, the prospect of a healthy marriage after living together is not a good one.

IS IT TOO LATE?

There is hope for the married couple who began their union by living together and is now experiencing disillusionment. But subtle relational habits and patterns don't change easily. The following suggestions, if conscientiously applied, can help restructure negative patterns.

1. Realize that the habit of emotional guardedness and distrust has been a part of the relationship from the beginning. It's important to recognize that this pattern has complicated normal marital conflicts by adding misunderstanding and overreactions.

2. Commit yourself to work through the complications created by your early relationship. Realize that this won't be a simple process. Distrust has been masquerading as intimacy. Vulnerability will include being honest about your feelings of fear and frustration while listening to and understanding your partner without attacking or escaping. This commitment is not a demand you make on your spouse, it's a decision you make for yourself.

3. Educate yourself about healthy marital communication

patterns. H. Norman Wright, James Dobson, and Gary Smalley are authors who can help you differentiate between what is normal, healthy, and productive, and what is defensive, reactive, and destructive. They will also help you develop new and more effective patterns of communication and conflict resolution in your marriage.

4. Consciously work on straightening out the double messages regarding commitment to your relationship. Do this by regularly affirming your trust in and love for one another. This is especially important during times of conflict and dissatisfaction. Remind your partner that you are committed to the relationship, even when the relationship isn't particularly enjoyable.

5. If you experience conflicts and negative feelings that you cannot resolve on your own, don't hesitate to find a professionally trained marriage counselor to help you work through them. Be sure to look for a therapist who shares your values and perspectives spiritually, morally, and relationally.

Relationships headed for destruction can be saved. The key factor is the couple's genuine desire to redirect their focus toward developing emotional and spiritual closeness. The road to resolution of marital issues will probably be neither short nor smooth. At this point, the relationship has brought the couple many painful struggles. Potentially, with courage and commitment, these experiences could lead both individuals to be more open than ever before as well as deepen their emotional bond in ways they never thought possible.

Growing closer

1. Go back and review your definition of intimacy from the "Growing Closer" section of chapter 2.

2. Which relationships in your life have fit that definition? If these are not current relationships, think about how they ended.

3. Are you aware of double messages or unspoken expectations that may have damaged intimacy or kept it from developing?

4. If you could relive those relationships, which of your own decisions and behaviors would you change and why?

If You Are Currently Unmarried and Living with Your Partner

1. Without discussion, each of you make a list of personal goals for the next three to five years. Be as detailed as possible. When your list is complete, sit together and share these goals. Discuss their implications for your relationship.
2. Make a list of reasons why you are not married to your partner and discuss these as a couple.

Karlyn's Thoughts
I Love You . . . I Think

Marriage. It's one of the happiest celebrations we know. I love going to weddings—the glowing bride, the grinning groom, the smiling families, everyone dressed in their best and ready to celebrate the biggest decision two people could ever make. Family and friends are excited with them, smiling to themselves as they remember everything this couple has been through—from the first time he took an hour to dial her number to the first time she came home squealing with news of the first kiss. Family was there to smooth out sizzling emotions after the fight that nearly broke them up, and friends were on hand to help him create the amazing proposal that made her cry. They've been there to wipe away tears, rationalize angry rampages, and laugh at how sappily in love these two are. Now all these people are in one place to support them as they step out in faith and trust, and promise to belong to each other for the rest of their lives. It's so beautiful.

And so totally terrifying.

Because, really, it *is* the biggest decision people make in their entire lives. I'm sure every bride and groom has their panicked, last-minute doubts: "*Oh no. What am I doing? Am I sure this is the right decision? What if he's not the one? What if she's not really all I want in a wife? What if Erick was really the one for me . . . ? What if Tiffany was really the right one . . . ? What if I haven't even met the one who was supposed to be the one. . . ? What if we're making a huge mistake and by next week we want to get divorced . . . ? What am I doing?*"

Good thing it's not any panicked thoughts at the altar that count. What really counts is the commitment that will let two people live out their lives together—*after* the celebration is over—as a successful team. It's that concrete decision that will let them be madly in love for the rest of their lives. Isn't that what marriage is all about? *That's* what makes me excited to be married—not the wedding itself but the deep commitment that comes into play *after* the wedding.

Since this marriage thing is one of the biggest commitments you'll ever make, doesn't it make sense to be absolutely sure it's the right decision before you make it? Of course it is. And the best way to make sure it's the right decision is to try it out first, right? Live together?

> *Hey, babe, so I was thinking . . . do you think it might be a good idea to try living together before we actually make a decision as big as marriage? Y'know . . . just to, um, see if we actually work? I mean, I love you and I'm pretty sure I want to be with you for the rest of my life . . . but . . . well, y'know. I don't want us to rush into anything without making sure we know what we're doing . . . y'know? I mean, we might as well try and save ourselves heartbreak later if things don't work out . . . better to find out that we won't last before marriage than after, huh? Heh heh . . . heh . . . ahem. So, um . . . whadd'ya think?*

Gee, how romantic.

What are some people really saying when they decide to live with their partners? Here's what I hear: "Look, I really feel like I love you, but I don't trust you to be responsible with my heart yet. You haven't quite won me over—there might be someone out there who would fit me better than you do. The time that I've spent dating you hasn't been sufficient to convince me that you'll love me forever, so I'm going to give you a chance to prove it to me now. If I don't get sick of living with you, then I suppose I won't get sick of being married to you. But I'm not giving any guarantees. This is a just a trial run. *If you fail, I will leave.*"

I have a feeling that if you listen closely and honestly, that's what you'll hear, too. Because a decision to live together may *feel* like it's a step of love and concern for the other person—and even a responsible step in making a bigger choice—but really it's a safety measure, wanting to have the physical benefits of living with someone you're deeply attracted to but not willing to stick to the tough commitment of a lifetime of love.

Cohabitation means a judgment based on *performance:* "What you do while we're living together is what I will base my decision on when deciding whether I want to be with you for the rest of my life."

On the other hand, marriage is a much bigger commitment than just living together. Marriage is saying, "I trust you with my heart. I'm risking *everything* in promising that for the rest of my life I'm going to love you, and you only. You now have the ability to flip my life upside down with just a decision to leave, but I'm trusting that your commitment to me is just as strong as my commitment to you. You're the only one there'll ever be for me. I'm placing myself in your hands, and until the day I die I will be forever exclusively yours."

Unlike cohabitation, in marriage there's no easy back door; if there comes a time when you don't like living with this person . . . tough. You've chosen to stick with it. You've decided to love this person. Unlike living together, marriage isn't a judgment based on performance; it's a decision to be unconditional in your love. No matter what this person does, you're going to love her or him for the rest of your lives. You're *determined* to love each other.

I know the two paragraphs you just read that contrast what cohabiting says versus what marriage says sound harsh and terrifying. But try looking at them a different way. Instead of looking at them as what you're saying to someone else, try hearing them from your boyfriend or girlfriend. Listen hard to what the person you love is saying to *you*. I'm not even going to ask which one you'd rather hear.

I'll tell you what *I'd* rather hear, though. Instead of that gibberish about saving me heartbreak and trying us out for a while, *this* is what I want to hear:

> *Karlyn, I love you. I can't imagine life without you next to me. You're my best friend. You've become a part of me, and I'm so thankful that God put you in my life. I don't deserve your love . . . but I never want to live without it. I never want to let you go again. I want to watch every single sunset with you. I want to wake up every morning and feel you there beside me. I want everyone to know that you're mine and that I love you with absolutely everything I have. I'm willing to spend the rest of my life learning how to love you better. It's not going to always be perfect or easy, but I'm ready to work at it. . . . I love you so much. . . . Will you marry me?*

Yeah, I know—I'm a romantic. But I'm also a realist. I've seen my friends try to find love by living together and end up completely ruining their lives. I've watched them halfway commit and then totally fall apart when they back out on their "commitment." Yes, marriage *is* a huge commitment. But it's a *whole* commitment. There are no ifs, ands, or buts; it's a total, complete, definite *I love you, and I will love you forever no matter what.*

No, it's not easy. Yes, living together is the quickest way to get the immediate perks without the hard work. But you know what? Talk to a couple who've been happily married for many years; they'll confirm that nothing will ever be worth as much as the rewards you get from sweating through the hard stuff in a marriage. And the perks you'll get from living together? Try looking at it this way: Your house is built on the edge of a steep ravine that has a good chance of eroding. Would you rather take the time to plant trees and plants that are going to dig their roots deep into the soil and keep the ground from dragging your house down the hill? Or would you rather pat some pretty leaves and branches over the top of the soil and smile at how green it looks? For everything in life—especially with decisions about your love life—the effort you put in determines the reward you'll get out. It's up to you.

4

The Illicit Effect

Remember Pavlov from your high school psychology days? He trained a dog to salivate in response to the ringing of a bell. Salivating was a physiological response stimulated by something not naturally associated with the response. In the same way, without realizing it, we can teach our bodies to react in ways they wouldn't normally. We call this process "conditioning."

With this in mind, we need to realize that sexual arousal can be conditioned very quickly, perhaps more readily than any other physiological response. The term *arousal* refers to the physical experience of excitement that surrounds the sexual experience—increased heart rate, increased blood pressure, tension, erection in males, and lubrication in females; all of these are physiological responses experienced during the process of sexual arousal.

An individual's repeated exposure to sexually stimulating material—pictures, books, films, objects, and countless other things—will affect or condition his or her sexual response. Arousal then becomes dependent upon what is known as a fetish—sexual excitement requiring a nonliving object as the focus of that arousal.

Randy's story provides a very sad but common illustration of this trap. Randy had grown up in a conservative Christian home with high moral values, but he became heavily involved in pornography prior to his marriage to Louise. Louise was an attractive woman in her early twenties who, like Randy, had come from a solid Christian home environment.

Randy had assumed that his desire for pornography would disappear when he and Louise were married. To Randy's dismay, he often had trouble becoming aroused by his new bride. More and more he found himself desiring, and even needing, to be exposed to some sort of pornography in order to function with her. At first he tried to hide his literature, but after several embarrassing experiences of being discovered, he gave up trying. Eventually he began subscribing to the Playboy channel on their cable TV, though he never watched it when Louise was around. Feeling increasingly guilty about his "habit," Randy soon stopped attending church with Louise as dissatisfaction in their relationship intensified.

Randy had developed a fetish for pornography without knowing it and certainly without intending to. For Randy the therapeutic process was a slow and emotionally painful one. Randy had to examine his deep feelings of inadequacy and fears of rejection. He also had to face his pattern of escaping into fantasy with imaginary sex partners, which made him dissatisfied with reality. These problems had developed over a period of years and would not change quickly. Faith, determination, honesty, forgiveness, and a mutual commitment by both Randy and Louise turned a very painful experience into regrettable history.

The fetish of illicitness

Participation in premarital sex creates a fetish similar to Randy's experience. Couples who are sexually active prior to marriage are conditioning themselves to respond to a fetish. The process is subtle. It can be, and often is, devastating to sexual enjoyment after marriage.

There is within each of us, especially those of us raised in a Judeo-Christian value system, an awareness that premarital sex is wrong. It may be deeply buried, repressed, ignored, or openly defied, but it's there. If we allow ourselves to listen to our feelings carefully and long enough, we will hear it. Something deep within us says, "We shouldn't be doing this . . . ," and there is something exciting about that. There's a stimulating quality in that wrongness. The term I use to describe this experience is *illicitness.*

Often our awareness of illicitness gets translated into self-talk—statements we make to ourselves—such as

- "What if someone finds out?"
- "I'll show my folks I can do what I want!"
- "See how much we love each other?"
- "No outdated church is going to control me!"

All of these reactions are revealing and reflect any number of experiences, including fear, defiance, shame, and control. The very nature of these justifications illustrates illicitness. We don't defend or rationalize an action that we honestly view as appropriate, and there's something inappropriate about premarital sex.

Besides generating a certain level of excitement, illicitness also fosters an emotional bond. This wrongness is something the couple shares. Even without discussion, it gives them a sense of being special and unique. This, of course, adds to the excitement and stimulation of illicitness.

How does a dating couple know if they are conditioning their sexual arousal to illicitness? There's no way to measure the impact of illicitness during courtship. If a couple is determined to rationalize, they'll probably do so successfully. The effect of illicitness, however, is very easily measured after the wedding.

I've talked with countless married couples, Christian and non-Christian alike, who have said to me, "Roger, before we were married we had a great sex life. It was exciting, fulfilling, enjoyable. But, for some reason, *on our wedding night* that excitement died. It's never been very good since."

What do you suppose happens to these couples on their wedding night? The illicitness, which has become conditioned (required sexual stimulus), has been taken away. Who will be offended or impressed by their behavior now? They are no longer proving something with their sexual relationship. Sex is now, in fact, mandatory for them since a well-adjusted marriage includes sexual interaction on a regular basis. The source of their sexual satisfaction has now dissolved and left confusion, disillusionment, and frustration in its place.

How does a person who has experienced the excitement of illicitness usually try to recapture it after he or she is married? One very simple method is to have an affair. Since there is also an awareness within each of us that extramarital sex is wrong, illicitness is a part of any adulterous relationship. The result? Marriages crumble, families are torn apart, and the divorce rate climbs.

Lost potential?

Let's further explore the effects of the illicitness trap. The better our understanding, the better equipped we'll be to avoid the trap as well as to help others avoid it.

Sexual enjoyment and responsiveness are always maximized by the absence of external tension. In other words, stress of any kind detracts from sexual fulfillment. Relaxation, contentment, and trust in both the environment and the relationship are extremely important variables for pleasure and enjoyment in the sexual experience.

A number of factors in most premarital sexual relationships intensify stress and minimize sexual fulfillment for both male and female:

1. The premarital sexual relationship fosters guilt and anxiety in both partners. The lack of a tangible, permanent commitment results in a level of insecurity.

    Beyond the sense of illicitness is fear of rejection. Since the relationship does not have the foundation of a lifetime commitment, each partner is likely to think, "He or she may not like how I am or what I do, or I may not be good enough." This results in preoccupation with one's performance and a fear of failure. Whenever people cannot abandon themselves completely to a partner in trust, confidence, and security, sexual satisfaction is minimized. This insecurity is often more intense for the woman. According to Dr. Helen Singer Kaplan, noted authority on sexual therapy,

> A trusting, loving relationship is important to insure sexual functioning. For a woman, a feeling of trust that the partner will meet her needs, particularly the dependency needs, and a feeling of security that the spouse will take care of her, will take responsibility for her, will not abandon her and will be loyal to her seem necessary in order to enable her to abandon herself to sexual pleasures. In fact, recent evidence indicates that trust may be one of the most important factors determining orgasmic capacity in women.[1]

2. Premarital sex is often hurried. Usually, the time or place is less than convenient. The need for gentle, patient stimulation as well as communication and expressions of love are neglected or altogether ignored. The caring part of the relationship tends to be set aside and the focus becomes personal physical satisfaction.

3. The goal of the male involved is usually physical release rather than sharing or meeting his partner's needs. Since female arousal is usually more gradual than that of the male, the focus is on his satisfaction. Many times she feels used or neglected, although this feeling is often repressed so the relationship can continue.

4. The premarital sexual experience is generally approached with little or no contraceptive preparation. The possibility of pregnancy brings with it a tension of its own. Talking about fears of pregnancy or discussing contraception is often avoided in dating relationships. Spontaneity ends up being prioritized above communication or planning.

5. Increased numbers of young people are facing the prospect of STDs. As the various STD epidemics escalate and public awareness increases, the tension and concern affects relationships

more significantly. It's now nearly universally accepted that the only effective protection against STDs is a lifetime commitment to one partner (monogamy).

All of these factors support the conclusion that premarital sex is never sex at its best. When a couple has forfeited the chance to experience sex within the secure relationship of a marriage commitment, they don't understand what they have given up. Unfortunately, they may never be able to experience sex at its best. They may never know what they could have experienced together had they been obedient to Scripture.

For the couple who may be thinking they should break up because their relationship is doomed, there is a ray of light. It is possible for an unmarried couple who has been sexually active to recapture that potential, at least to some degree. But it doesn't happen by accident; it's accomplished through conscious decisions and commitment. It means ending all sexual intercourse and setting some clear limits on the physical relationship for a period of time prior to the wedding (the longer the better). Together, the couple must make serious decisions about how to handle their natural sexual temptations so that appropriate patterns can be established. Chapter 8 discusses how a couple goes about restructuring their physical relationship.

For the married couple who recognize and understand these patterns—and the consequences for their marriage—several steps will help begin the process of positive change. Some of the issues you'll need to discuss together may feel awkward or threatening at first, but it's important to talk about them despite this feeling. Relationship growth seldom occurs in a marriage without direct communication.

1. Set aside time to be alone as a couple and discuss your early sexual patterns. Share what you would have liked to change in your courtship. Be sure to think about and explain why these changes would have been important. At the end of this chapter is a section designed to help begin the conversation.

2. Admit and discuss with one another the mistakes you made in

courtship. Also talk about your understanding of the impact of those mistakes on your current relationship.

3. Make a decision to forgive both your partner and yourself for the past. Forgiveness means no longer requiring payment for the wrongs committed against you. In relationships these "payments" can take many forms: withdrawal, silence, angry outbursts, brooding resentment, and lack of cooperation. Forgiveness may not miraculously change the relationship, but without forgiveness there can be no real change.

4. Learn to discuss openly your sexual relationship with one another. What are your desires, preferences, dreams, and fears? This may not be a single conversation but many conversations over a long period of time.

5. Read and discuss the following books:

    • *Re-Bonding* by Donald Joy[2]
    • *Intended for Pleasure* by Ed Wheat and Gaye Wheat[3]

6. If, after taking these steps, you both feel little progress toward the changes you desire, consider finding a professional marriage counselor or family therapist who shares your values. Your pastor, priest, or rabbi may be helpful in locating one.

Growing closer

Draw a line from the physical level on the left to what you believe to be the appropriate commitment level on the right.

Physical Level	Commitment Level
Holding Hands	Casual Relationship
Hugging	
Kissing	First Date
French Kissing	
Caressing, above the neck	Steady Dating
Caressing, below the neck	
Petting (Underneath clothing, no sexual organs)	Exclusive Dating
Petting (Underneath clothing, sexual organs)	Engagement
Sexual Intercourse	
	Marriage

1. How do your beliefs expressed in this exercise actually apply to your relationships?
2. If you are dating or are engaged, how does your opinion on the above exercise compare to your partner's opinion? Try having him or her do the same exercise before you share your responses. (You may learn a lot about how well you know each other.)
3. How do differences in these areas affect a courtship relationship?

For Those Who Are Married

Take some time to complete the following statements as honestly and thoroughly as you can. After completing them individually, share your responses and discuss your feelings about them.

1. If I could change one thing from our courtship, it would be _____.
2. The reason I would have made this change is _____.
3. A change I can make in this area now is _____.
4. The thing I most appreciate about our sexual relationship is _____.
5. For me, the most helpful change in our sexual relationship would be _____.
6. Some things I can do to facilitate this change are _____.
7. Something I think you could do to help this change is _____.

Karlyn's Thoughts
What You Know Will Hurt You

Put yourself in this story. You're fourteen. You're the youngest kid of five, and all your older siblings have taught you bits and pieces about driving so you're *dying* to try it. One night you and a friend sneak out at two in the morning and take your older brother's beat-up old Chevy truck down to the school parking lot. Your heart is thumping and your breath is coming in gulps, but you've never had so much fun in your entire life! After a couple of hours looping around the parking lot, then pulling e-brake turns, and then barreling over curbs and parking blocks, you feel like a pro. As you return the truck to the driveway you're so nervous that your brother is going to catch you that you think you're going to throw up. But he doesn't, you don't, and all is well.

A couple of weeks later you want to go driving again so badly you can *taste* it. Now you feel like you can actually do it—no more practicing needed. So you call up a couple of friends and, again at two in the morning, all three of you sneak out and this time take your mom's beloved Toyota Camry around the neighborhood. Again, you're so ter-rified that you'll be caught or that something will go wrong, you feel every beat of your heart for the entire hour and a half. But, again, you've never had so much fun! This is even better than last time.

Pretty soon this becomes a routine. Every few weeks you and a couple of friends will sneak out in the night with someone's car and go somewhere new. Each time there's that nervous excite-ment—something could go even a little wrong and you'd all be in *huge* trouble—but it's worth it. Eventually you've driven every car at your house several times over—from your sister's old beater Ford to your dad's brand-new Jaguar. Every time you drive by a cop you get so nervous you think you're going to pass out—but you've never been stopped. There *was* that one time that your oldest sister caught you sneaking back into the house after you'd used her car. She was angry, and when Mom and Dad found out, they weren't exactly pleased either. They grounded you for so long you were afraid you'd never see the light of day again. But getting caught didn't deter you from doing it again . . . and again . . . and again. . . . Now there's an added danger of what *could* happen if something went wrong again, and it's exhilarating—almost intoxicating. You just can't stay away from it.

Finally, you turn sixteen. You've got your license. Your parents buy you a car and hand over the keys. You're so excited to *finally* be able to drive your *own* car—and in the daylight!—that you rush right out and tear out of the driveway. Laughing, you pick up your friends and you zip down the freeway like so many times before.

But . . . something's missing. This should be one of the most excit-ing days of your life—but there isn't any excitement. There *is*, but it's not the same. You're happy, but you're not intoxicated with the thrill of it all. Your heart isn't up in your throat. There's no danger involved to make you giddy with exhilaration. There's no reason to sneak around anymore . . . no reason to use another person's car . . . no reason to freak out every time a cop passes you. Where's the fun in *that?* Sud-denly, now that all your forbidden actions are allowed, the fun has been sucked out of them. You've lost the thrill of driving your own car because it's boring. You *do*, however, taste some of that old excitement when you take your *friends'* new cars out for a spin. . . .

What do you think would have happened the day you got your own car if you'd never driven a car by yourself before? The first time your dad handed you the keys to your *very own car,* you'd be beside yourself with nervous energy. Your heart would pound in your throat, and you'd be terrified and excited and confident all at the same time. The thrill of being trusted to head out on the open roads all by yourself would be intoxicating. You'd be in control, driving your very own car without someone next to you telling you what to do! That heady feeling, of course, wouldn't last until the day you die, but you'd never be disappointed by the lack of thrill in driving. What's there to be lacking? You wouldn't know any different. It would always be enjoyable because *nothing would be missing.* Everything would be just like it's supposed to be.

Now consider what it's like when you experience sex before you get married. The thrill of being able to do whatever you want, whenever you want, with *whomever* you want is intoxicating. It's thrilling. Something in the back of your mind tells you that you're free to do whatever you want no matter what anyone says, and you've got an exciting sense of control. You can manipulate the system. You are the *man.* You are the *woman.*

But then, when you finally decide to tie the knot, something goes horribly wrong. The magic, the thrill—it's gone. What you once did without asking anyone's permission, you now do with *everyone's* permission. Where's the fun in *that?* You feel the lack of the illicit thrill, and sex with your spouse is no longer exciting, no longer fulfilling. You long for what you once had—the tingly exhilaration that this experience used to hold for you. Who wants to do something that feels boring when you *know* it could be exciting? Now, sneaking around with someone *else* brings that old excitement back. . . .

Can you see the correlation? When you teach yourself to love and need the excitement of secrecy, and then that secrecy no longer exists, the excitement will disappear. But if you never train yourself to need that, you'll never be missing something. When you sleep with your spouse you can get excited *every single time,* because you don't need to be doing something *illicit* to be having fun. What do you think you'd rather have? Lots of great exhilaration now and years of dissatisfaction later on, or the tough choice of self-denial now and a fulfilling, thrilling sex life after you're married?

I'm thankful that I'll never miss the feeling of illicit sex because I won't know what it feels like. I've chosen to wait, and for a long time, if necessary. As exciting as going all the way now could be, the feeling doesn't last. And if I had to feel something missing from my sex life for the *rest* of my life, I'd rather not know what I'd missed. I'd much rather be naive and unpracticed. I don't want to feel like my old boyfriends were better sex partners than my husband. I want to be so impressed with him that I can hardly stand it. He *is* going to be the most exciting thing I will ever experience—because I won't know anything different.

What will *you* choose to experience?

5

The Technical Virginity Trap

A few years ago I addressed a youth leadership conference on the topic of sexuality for Christians. Following one of the workshops a young woman asked a pertinent question. I well remember the situation because every unmarried person present leaned forward and nodded their approval of the question. I had obviously left out something important from my talk.

"I've recently gotten engaged. My fiancé and I have worked hard to keep our relationship sexually pure. But we have strong feelings for each other, and we're very affectionate. After hearing what you've said today, something confuses me. Can petting be damaging to a relationship, or are we just talking about sleeping together?"

Her question was a good one and deserved a direct answer. The answer, however, is more complex than just yes or no. I hope I was able to give her an adequate answer in the short time we had that day. This chapter will answer that same sticky question as thoroughly as possible.

Petting is a difficult term to define clearly. Certainly petting involves two individuals touching one another in some sensual manner, but that may be the only common element in many definitions. Some definitions revolve around which parts of the body are caressed. Many definitions will describe petting in terms of two levels: "light petting," which usually means the couple is clothed, and "heavy petting," which usually means the couple is undressed. For our purposes, petting is mutual stimulation without sexual intercourse, or coitus, as its goal. It involves building sexual tension through fondling another person's sexually sensitive areas without relieving that tension through intercourse. Petting may or may not involve orgasm.

If we think of sexual behavior on a continuum from holding hands to coitus, petting could be described as more intense than a kiss and hug, but less intense than intercourse. Because of the arousal of sexual desire, many couples who intend to go no further than petting will, of course, end up having intercourse. When a couple intends to have intercourse, this type of fondling is called "foreplay." So in this sense, the only difference between petting and foreplay is one of intention.

Some people think petting is a way for two people who care for one another and value their virginity to give each other sexual pleasure without going all the way. They think it's a way for two people who are committed to each other, although unmarried, to begin emotional preparation for a sexual relationship without violating the biblical code of sexual abstinence. Others recognize that petting is a type of defrauding because it arouses desires and fantasies that cannot be morally fulfilled. They realize that however much the individuals care for each other, they are creating a bond meant only for marriage— without any guarantee they will remain together.

The Progression

A natural progression develops in sexual stimulation and arousal— from something as subtle as a smile to something as powerful as intercourse. It includes holding hands, kissing, caressing, fondling, and many stages in between. The common denominator in all these behaviors is the direction. That direction is to intensify, increase, and progress.

With time, however, each stage becomes less and less satisfying. Once you progress from hand-holding to kissing, it's extremely difficult to return to only hand-holding without a feeling of dissatisfaction. Our physiological sensations urge us toward intercourse. That's not a bad thing necessarily; within the commitment of marriage it's an incredibly exciting and emotionally strengthening bond. Outside of that commitment, those urges can be a lot like quicksand.

Emotional intimacy emerges through identifiable stages of contact. Each of these stages is an essential component in the development toward the "emotional covenant" of becoming husband and wife. The sense of oneness derived from this covenant is what gives a healthy marriage relationship its almost mystical uniqueness among all other relationships. These stages of contact nurture a special bond of companionship that draws two people together as no other relationship can. In his book *Intimate Behavior,* well-known British zoologist/anthropologist Desmond Morris describes in depth the patterns of human intimacy. I have paraphrased and abridged his findings on courtship patterns:

1. *Eye to Body.* A glance reveals so much about a person—sex, size, shape, age, personality, and status. The importance people place on these criteria determines whether they will be attracted to each other.

2. *Eye to Eye.* When the man and woman who are strangers to each other exchange glances, their most natural reaction is to look away, usually with embarrassment. If their eyes meet again, they may smile, which signals that they may like to become better acquainted.

3. *Voice to Voice.* Their initial conversations are trivial and include questions like "What's your name?" or " What do you do for a living?" During this long stage the two people learn much about each other's opinions, pastimes, activities, habits, hobbies, likes, and dislikes. If they're compatible, they become friends.

4. *Hand to Hand.* The first instance of physical contact between the couple is usually a nonromantic occasion such as when the man helps the woman descend a high step or aids her across an obstacle. At this point, each of the individuals can withdraw from the relationship without rejecting the other.

If continued, however, hand-to-hand contact will eventually become an evidence of the couple's romantic attachment to each other.

5. *Hand to Shoulder.* This affectionate embrace is still noncommittal. It is a "buddy" type position in which the man and woman are side by side. They are more concerned with the world in front of them than they are with each other. The hand-to-shoulder contact reveals a relationship that is more than a close friendship, but probably not real love.

6. *Arm to Waist.* Because this is something two people of the same sex would not ordinarily do, it is clearly romantic. They are close enough to be sharing secrets or intimate language with each other. Yet, as they walk side by side with hand to waist, they are still facing forward.

7. *Face to Face.* This level of contact involves gazing into each other's eyes, hugging, and kissing. If none of the previous stages were skipped, the man and woman will have developed a special code from experience that enables them to engage in communication with very few words. At this point, sexual desire becomes an important factor in the relationship.

8. *Hand to Head.* This is an extension of the previous stage. The man and woman tend to cradle or stroke each other's head while kissing or talking. Rarely do individuals in our culture touch the head of another person unless the two are either romantically involved or are family members. It is a designation of emotional closeness.

9.–12. *The Final Steps.* The last four levels of involvement are distinctly sexual and private. They are (9) hand to body, (10) mouth to breast, (11) touching below the waist, and (12) intercourse.[1]

It's impossible to overemphasize the importance of moving through each of these stages slowly and systematically. True intimacy between a man and a woman grows gradually and gently. Time and patience are essential—the two aspects of courtship that cannot be rushed. When a couple moves too quickly or skips a stage, the natural emotional bonding process is disrupted and something is lost in the development of the emotional partnership between them.

As these twelve stages illustrate, the progression is toward genital-to-genital bonding, or intercourse. A couple who wants to avoid intercourse before marriage, who does not feel ready for a marriage commitment, and yet who is involved in petting has few options open besides failure or frustration. The couple is attempting to pursue and intensify a natural progression, only to abort it just prior to fulfillment.

This natural progression is the force that pushes a couple who have had intercourse to continue having it—even if they feel guilty about it. This progression is also what compels a person who has had intercourse in one relationship to pursue it in the next, even when he or she knows it was a problem in the previous relationship.

For most couples, petting is like shifting a car into high gear—it generally speeds up the progression toward coitus. The pursuit of physical pleasure dominates the relationship, and emotional growth and communication often come to a screeching halt.

Couples who are in the petting stage generally don't talk much, at least not in depth. They neglect the exploration of each other's personalities in favor of exploring physical sensations. While the physical aspect escalates, the relationship stagnates. They give more and more attention and energy to being alone together and to satisfying their physical appetites. They spend less and less time being social with other people or with each other. The date becomes a time to get through in order to arrive at the real agenda for the evening—physical stimulation and arousal.

Before long, very little is left in the relationship besides physical involvement. Feeling close is dependent upon physical contact, and giving it up feels like giving up the relationship. Sexual compulsion is almost inevitable. If a couple isn't willing to risk the loss of the relationship by backing away from physical intimacy, or if they just don't give it much thought, sex dominates the relationship even without intercourse.

Often the person who has the most difficulty controlling the progression is the one with a deep need to be loved. This is a person who feels unloved, perhaps unlovable, and may be afraid on a deep level that he or she doesn't have anything to contribute to a relationship. The person who is searching to fill a void left by an affection-starved past is extremely susceptible to misreading relationship signals and often translates another person's selfish lust into a message of genuine love.

While the potential for this type of vulnerability is always present, most people would agree that physical involvement is a pitifully poor substitute for genuine love and caring. Tim Stafford, who regularly provides a practical, biblical perspective on love and sex in a question-and-answer column for *Campus Life* magazine, puts it this way:

> In our culture, couples who have been going together for a while are likely to hug, kiss and hold hands. I think these are, for most people, warm and innocent ways to express loving appreciation. When you go further and aim for sexual excitement, I think you generally stop speaking the language of love. Why? Because you have to stop somewhere short of intercourse. Some people can't—they lose control. Some people lose the desire to stop. Some people keep control, but they do so at the cost of feeling frustrated. Instead of feeling warm toward each other, they feel overheated. I have never known this to help a relationship to grow, especially when people spend hours together revving up their motors and pushing the brakes at the same time. You'd be a lot better off just talking and getting to know each other.[2]

Chapter 4 discussed the trap of illicitness, that is, the process of conditioning an individual's sexual response to inappropriate stimuli. We can't discuss the dangers involved in petting without dealing with illicitness, because the same principles apply. Any time sexual arousal is pursued for its own sake, as is generally the case with petting, the potential for problematic conditioning exists. If it's been awhile since you read the chapter on illicitness, you may want to go back and refresh your memory on the main points of the conditioning process before completing this chapter.

If petting is used to bolster a person's poor self-esteem, then self-esteem will soon come to depend upon petting. If petting is used to feel close to another person, it will be difficult to feel close without petting. We just can't separate the phenomenon of conditioning from sexual arousal. We can only structure our sexual relationships so that we are conditioning appropriate arousal responses. We don't do that in just one or two experiences, we do it over the long haul. We do it by thoughtfully developing a relationship that is consistent with our values and goals.

The Biblical perspective

What does the Bible say about petting? It is commonly assumed that young people in biblical times reached puberty at a somewhat later age than young people do today. The difference is usually attributed to the improved diet and medical care children have today. Whatever the reason, the average age of puberty of biblical young people was probably about fourteen or fifteen. Marriage probably occurred at about the same age, so there was not much need to deal with sexual tension outside of marriage. Contact between the sexes was also limited. Generally boys attended school while girls didn't, and marriages were arranged by parents. Also, a young person's sexual contact was closely guarded by the parents because a daughter's virginity strongly affected her father's dowry, or "bride price." Thus, a father had financial reasons to protect his daughter's purity before marriage.

Circumstances are different for young people today. From the time they are very young, boys and girls are usually not segregated. They spend a great deal of time together. The average age of puberty is younger today, usually twelve or thirteen. The average age of marriage in the United States is much older, twenty-three to twenty-five. This gives young people a period of sexual maturity and sexual tension that rarely existed 2,000 years ago. It also creates many opportunities to experiment with sexual relationships—rare in biblical times.

Physical desire and contact naturally increase as a couple moves closer to a marriage commitment. As sexual passion builds, perspective is distorted—good intentions are often lost in the rush of emotions and physical sensations. Motives can quickly change from benevolence to self-gratification, from affection to lust. And when your goal becomes sexual excitement instead of an appropriate expression of love and commitment, you've entered a danger zone that often results in the destruction of a healthy, growing relationship.

Does the Bible say that petting is right or wrong? While many passages are clear regarding sexual intercourse outside of marriage, other sexual behaviors such as petting aren't discussed directly. But we can clearly discern God's viewpoint from passages that deal with lust and self-discipline:

> You have heard that it was said, "Do not commit adultery." But I tell you that anyone who looks at a woman lustfully has already committed adultery with her in his heart. (Matthew 5:27–28)

Jesus is pointing out that sins can be committed in the heart even if outward behavior doesn't carry out that sin.

> Now to the unmarried and the widows I say: It is good for them to stay unmarried, as I am. But if they cannot control themselves, they should marry, for it is better to marry than to burn with passion. (1 Corinthians 7:8–9)

> Flee from youthful lusts, and pursue righteousness, faith, love and peace, with those who call on the Lord from a pure heart. (2 Timothy 2:22 NASB)

> Flee from sexual immorality. All other sins a man commits are outside his body, but he who sins sexually sins against his own body. Do you not know that your body is a temple of the Holy Spirit, who is in you, whom you have received from God? You are not your own; you were bought at a price. Therefore honor God with your body. (1 Corinthians 6:18–20)

The message is clear—it is a warning sign with flashing lights and blaring sirens. God is telling us to run as fast as we can from sexual impurity. He is saying there is extreme danger in fostering sexual thoughts and intentions outside of a marriage relationship.

How, then, should a single person handle sexual desire? How can a person take the guesswork out of what is right and wrong sexual behavior? Author Michael Crosby says it well:

> From Jesus' viewpoint, all of life should be governed by a deep love for God and other people. Instead of determining what to do in each of our daily decisions by reflecting upon what is required by some law, Jesus would ask, "What is the most ethical and loving thing I could do in this situation?" His focus was upon what is right, not upon what is legal. The question for him was not "What can I get away with in order to gratify my own desires?" but "How can I best serve God and give of myself to help others?" Life lived on the level of manipulation is in actuality subhuman, a cheap imitation of real life. The idea of two people using each other to satisfy their physical appetites would be repugnant to Jesus and the Apostle Paul. They would assert that selfish living is truncated living, that pleasure gained through using others is only a pitiful shadow of the real joy involved in giving yourself unselfishly for another and happily receiving back what that person gives to you. This is not at all to diminish sexual desire or pleasure but to put them in their rightful place. Sex should be an enjoyable part of married life.[3]

For an unmarried couple, another option is available besides breaking up or allowing sexual compulsion to dominate. That option is starting over. It means going back and resetting priorities and goals and deciding how to grow through the stages of physical involvement listed earlier in this chapter, reserving the intimacies of steps 9–12 for marriage. Starting over is a difficult process. It takes a lot of commitment, and many relationships don't survive the tension. But if the goal of the relationship is marriage, it's well worth the effort. The fact is, if the relationship can't survive this kind of restructuring of priorities and behavior, it certainly won't survive the rigors of fifty years of life together.

petting without a partner

Another area of technical virginity is sexual self-stimulation, or masturbation. It's an uncomfortable topic loaded with guilt and fear. It's amazing, though, that any time I speak to a group of young people and ask them to write down anonymous questions for me, I can guarantee that masturbation will come up many times. It's a big question on the minds of most single people.

In the past, masturbation was blamed for everything from homosexuality to insanity, from laziness to hairy knuckles. Considering the way this topic has been addressed in past generations, it's not surprising that most people are uncomfortable even mentioning the word.

Masturbation is defined as manipulating one's own body in such a way as to arouse sexual tension. It is having sex without a partner and may or may not include orgasm. The physical sensation of arousal and release can occur with no relationship to another person.

Scriptural Silence

As in the case of petting, the Bible does not specifically mention masturbation. Genesis 38:8–10 is typically used to teach that God doesn't approve of masturbation. The biggest problem with using it for that reason is that masturbation wasn't involved. Onan had intercourse with his brother's widow as required by the Levirate law of inheritance; the situation was not one of self-stimulation. His problem was not a sexual one but a direct violation of God's command.

The purpose of this particular law was to assure that the Hebrew lineage was carried on. It was a disaster when a man died without fathering children. To avoid this, the law commanded that the dead man's brother marry the widow and that their children be raised as offspring of the deceased. The children would inherit his property and carry on his name (Deut. 25:5–6).

Onan violated this law. He had intercourse with his brother's widow, but withdrew before orgasm and ejaculated onto the ground, doing so in order to avoid producing children for his brother. Onan was punished, not for masturbating, but for violating God's law. So the one passage generally used as an example of masturbation in the Bible isn't an example of masturbation at all. The reason this passage is used so often as a stricture against masturbation is because there are no others. Scripture does, however, specifically denounce lust and any behavior that would promote or reinforce impure thoughts.

Dangers of Self-Stimulation

For the teenager who has the sexual urges of adulthood but is in no way ready for a marriage commitment, self-stimulation for sexual release would appear to be a natural phase of sexual development that is left behind as meaningful relationships are developed with the opposite sex. For adults who, for various reasons, remain single, masturbation would appear to serve the same purpose. After all, it is sexual gratification without the complications of pregnancy, disease, or rejection.

But if it were this simple, there would be no struggle with the feelings of loneliness, emptiness, and guilt that are usually associated with masturbation. These are feelings that seem to describe most people's emotional responses to self-stimulation. The feelings of emptiness and isolation shouldn't surprise us when we consider God's purpose for sex—a relationship created as the expression of a lifelong bond between two committed and loving individuals. Masturbation, then, is a replacement for a relationship. It is an inadequate substitute for sexual oneness with a life partner.

Although it's foolish to assume masturbation can satisfy one's need to be close to another person, neither should it be a source of self-hatred. Many issues in life are worth struggling over, such as our concept of God and our relationship to Him, our forgiveness of others, and our concept of our own worth. We must not magnify the issue of masturbation out of proportion. A good measurement for an individual struggling over the rightness or wrongness of masturbation is the question, Does it promote lust?

There are dangers in sexual self-stimulation, and those that may not be obvious on the surface need to be discussed. They relate to self-stimulation as a habit, and they are problems for the individual both now and for his or her future marriage relationship.

Compulsivity

Consider the hypothetical case of John, a twenty-two-year-old single Christian man. John is rather unsure of himself socially. Although he's competent and successful as a computer programmer and is well accepted in his small circle of friends, he struggles with self-doubt and low self-esteem. As a result of these feelings, John tends to be shy and withdrawn in relationships and has never dated steadily. John compulsively masturbates to orgasm two to three times daily. He is deeply ashamed of his habit but feels powerless to stop.

John has found a temporary escape from his negative emotions through sexual self-stimulation. In this pattern of escape, a cycle is established that leads to a literal addiction to masturbation. This cycle is illustrated below:

painful feelings of failure, loneliness, fear, self-doubt

self-stimulation giving pleasant sensation and avoiding bad feelings

resulting feelings of guilt and self-condemnation

As the diagram illustrates, the compulsion begins with John's poor self-concept and his desire for an escape from negative feelings. The escape is temporary, of course, and results in deeper feelings of failure, which lead him to escape again into pleasant sensations.

Resolution for John will not lie in increased self-discipline—gritting his teeth and fighting the urge to masturbate—but in learning to view himself as an adequate person, worthy of being loved. Part of the solution will involve learning to establish appropriate, healthy relationships with women. He needs to let other people meet his emotional needs and accept the risks of building relationships. As he does this, John will probably find his compulsion to masturbate lessening until this ineffective and inappropriate method of receiving nurturance is replaced by more satisfying relationships with other people.

Poor Sexual Habits

Jim married Peggy when he was twenty-seven. Prior to his marriage he masturbated several times a week for sexual release. Jim didn't feel good about this practice, but it clearly wasn't an obsession with him. Since it wasn't affecting his life in any negative way, he didn't give it much thought. After their marriage, however, the newlyweds found themselves in a frustrating dilemma. It was clear that Jim had a serious problem with premature ejaculation. He found it extremely difficult to delay his ejaculation long enough for Peggy to be sexually satisfied. Frequently Jim would ejaculate during foreplay. The resulting frustration and embarrassment caused serious problems in their young marriage. Although he didn't realize it at the time, Jim's problem was the result of his earlier masturbation pattern.

A man and a woman generally do not reach orgasm at the same pace. A common struggle, especially for new husbands, is to slow down their arousal process in order to allow their wives also to reach a climax. An individual who has masturbated consistently has developed some bad habits, the reason being that in self-stimulation there are no considerations other than one's own satisfaction. Since the purpose is sexual release, the goal in masturbation is usually to reach a climax as quickly as possible. This commonly results in a pattern of premature ejaculation after marriage.

Premature ejaculation is seldom considered a serious sexual dysfunction and is not difficult to treat in therapy. It can, however, be extremely frustrating to a couple and can be the source of miscommunication and resentment. Premarital sexual intercourse, because of its focus on self-satisfaction, often results in the same problem of premature ejaculation. Women who masturbate compulsively frequently experience inhibited sexual arousal.

The Acceleration Problem

Another hazard of masturbation is inherent in almost all sexual activity—the tendency to increase the behavior the more it is practiced. In other words, the more you do it, the more you want it. Masturbation doesn't function as a release of sexual pressure in the long run; actually it is just the opposite. While an individual may experience some release of sexual pressure immediately following masturbation, sexual activity generally leads to increased sexual drive. So self-stimulation, as with other sexual activities such as intercourse or petting, tends to draw the individual toward more activity.

If the goal is to reduce pressure, it would be more helpful to redirect one's mental and emotional focus to some other interest. This means looking outward, developing relationships—male and female—that are healthy and close, but not sexual. It also means developing interests and hobbies that build self-esteem, self-satisfaction, and a feeling of success. Most important, it means avoiding exposure to sexually arousing material: pornographic literature, sexually suggestive television or movies, and other materials that cause heightened sexual desire. In our present culture it's probably unrealistic to think we can totally eliminate such input from our lives. A great deal can be avoided, however, through a little effort. In the long run, the preceding suggestions are more effective ways of reducing sexual pressure than is masturbation.

Let me summarize what I've said about issues of masturbation:

• Don't be consumed with self-condemnation. While masturbation is far from the best expression of sexual bonding, it is
not the unforgivable sin. It will not make you mentally ill, lazy,
or homosexual.

• Masturbation will not resolve your feelings of loneliness, fear,
or inadequacy. It is not a substitute for relational closeness.

• Indiscriminate practice of masturbation may lead to physical
and mental habits that will need to be broken in order to enjoy
a healthy marriage relationship.

• Masturbation is not a shortcut to anything; it is short-term
sexual release without a partner.

Maintaining technical virginity, whether through petting or masturbation, is often destructive and never helpful to a developing relationship. Both behaviors promote confusion, frustration, and guilt, especially
in those who want to follow the biblical standard of sexual purity.

If you had eight o'clock reservations at a four-star restaurant, would
you go to a fast-food drive-in at seven o'clock? Most likely you wouldn't
want to spoil your appetite; you'd consider the enjoyment and ceremony of dinner at the fancy restaurant well worth the wait.

Similarly, God has given "four stars" to marriage, and He has designed us so that we can be fulfilled only within its exclusivity.

growing closer

1	2	3	4	5	6	7	8	9	10

Extremely   **Perfectly**
uncomfortable   **at peace**

1. Place an X on the scale to indicate how comfortable you are, or
   have been in the past, with your physical relationships with
   the opposite sex.

2. Where do you think your partner would place his or her mark?

3. What specific changes would need to take place in order for you to place your mark on 10?
4. How would you go about making those changes?

Karlyn's Thoughts
Standard Decision

Use your imagination for a second. Put yourself into the future and imagine yourself sitting on your couch with your future husband or wife. *Not* the person you're dating now. Just imagine that all your current plans fall through and you *don't* end up marrying the person you're dating—or are even engaged to—now. The person you're sitting next to in your mind is your husband or wife. You're so in love with that person, you can't believe you ever thought you were in love with anyone else. This relationship has been right from the beginning, and now you're going to spend the rest of your lives with each other. But there's something that you have to do first.

You have to tell that person what you've done with every other person you've ever dated.

Everything.

Does that prospect make you nervous? Sick, maybe? The reason that technical virginity is an issue in Christian relationships is because even though people understand that they're supposed to save sex for marriage, everything that leads up to intercourse is so much fun that it's not exciting to save it until later. It's too hard. It takes too much work to deny each other pleasure that you both want. Is it really worth it? Your answer to that question depends upon what your standard for physical involvement is. Do you know what your standard is? Is it something like this: "Uh . . . I dunno . . . whatever feels right . . ."? It's hard to find a standard for limiting physical intimacy. I know, I've tried every standard I could think of. I've tried not kissing until I was engaged (didn't make it), adhering to a set of rules (didn't work), stopping when we felt it was too much (didn't happen), and doing whatever felt *right* at the time (keep dreaming). The good news is that I finally found a standard that *does* work; the not-so-good news is that it takes a lot of effort and determination on both sides. Here's the standard: When you have to look your wife or husband in the eye and tell him or her what you did with someone else, what would you feel good about revealing? *That's* what you can do. There's your standard.

Sound difficult? It is. But most of us are eventually going to promise our lives to someone. You're going to want to love that person with everything you have; not everything you have *left*. You'll promise to belong to that person for the rest of your life—your body actually *belongs* to someone! If you look at it that way, you're only *on loan* to whomever you're dating right now. The respect you deserve isn't just for you but also for your future spouse. "In this same way, husbands ought to love their wives as their own bodies. He who loves his wife loves himself. . . . 'For this reason a man will leave his father and mother and be united to his wife, and the two will become one flesh'" (Eph. 5:28, 31). You're going to *become one flesh* with your husband or wife. The person who sins sexually against you is sinning against your future spouse as well.

Isn't that incentive enough to guard yourself and your boyfriend or girlfriend a bit more tomorrow night? Think about it this way. Girls, do you want to look your future husband in the eye and tell him whose body you let lay on top of yours at two o'clock in the morning while you made out? Guys, do you want to explain to your future wife why you touched another girl's breasts or slipped your tongue into another woman's mouth?

The standard I've suggested here isn't the easiest to keep. In order for you to succeed, you've got to commit, as a couple, to work together and do—or don't do—whatever's necessary to make it happen. Whatever that looks like will depend on you, but here's something that's been invaluable to me: go to a Christian couple you respect, preferably a couple in the ministry, and ask them to keep the two of you accountable. Go to them regularly for advice. Keep the lines of communication totally open with them—and with each other. Talk to each other *all the time*, about *everything* you're thinking. *Decide not to lie.* Don't hide from your mentors anything that you're doing. If you have to lie about what's going on, you *know* it's wrong. But the most important thing is to determine to love the person you're dating so much that you want to protect his or her future above your desire for pleasure. It's called *real* love.

What if you've messed up in the past and you're already sick about what you would have to describe to your future spouse? *Start over today.* It's not too late. You're not a failure, even if you've done "everything but"—or even everything—in all your previous relationships and in your current relationship. *God can make you clean again.* He's as eager to help you succeed as he is to help the person who's never even kissed anyone. You, however, have the harder job. You have to put your past in the past and keep it there. You've decided to become a new person and the old person is not a part of who you are anymore. Yes, you're going to have to show that to your husband or wife later on, but you'll be able to tell that person that you started over because your love for them put him or her above all your other dating relationships.

Here's what your biggest temptation will be: you'll want to say, "Well, I've already done that with so-and-so, so it's not like I'll be saving anything I haven't already given away." *Don't do that!* You're a new person, you've got a second chance, and everything's new again! Yes, it's going to be harder for you because you know what you're missing, but your reward will be that much sweeter as you overcome the temptations.

What's the reward for all this? The triumph of beating your own demons. The elation you'll feel when you look back and see what you've come through. The inner strength born only of victory that will last far longer than a single night of pleasure. You already know the pain that comes of giving too much of yourself away. You don't have to go through that again. Struggling with and *beating* this kind of temptation is going to be far more satisfying than those fleeting pleasures.

Are you willing to make this decision? Are you willing to commit to this standard? How you answer could determine whether your relationships live well . . . or die hard.

6

sexual addiction

This chapter is not about sinful behavior, although sinful behavior will be discussed. It's not about overindulgence in sex, although sex is certainly involved. This chapter is about a sickness of mind and spirit that by its very nature keeps people from getting well. Unlike a physical illness, in this illness the affected individual is personally responsible for both the symptoms and the cure. It's a sickness to which Christians are not immune. It's an addiction—an addiction to lust. Both men and women are equally subject to sexual addiction, but I've chosen to use the pronouns *he* and *him* in this chapter only to preserve sentence continuity.

Think about chemical addiction for a moment. When an individual is addicted to alcohol or some other drug, that drug becomes a preoccupation. The addict will go to great lengths to satisfy his craving for it. The substance will become more important than family, friends, or work. Eventually, the drug is needed to feel normal. The addict's life becomes unmanageable as important relationships are sacrificed for the addiction.

Now transfer this concept of addiction into the sexual area, and we're talking about sexual addiction. A clinical definition is "a pathological relationship with a mood-altering experience which becomes the central focus of attention."[1] An addict's judgment is significantly impaired and he pursues his addiction in spite of serious negative consequences.

just oversexed?

Before Steve was married, his reputation was that of a playboy. He was handsome and athletic and had no trouble finding women who wanted to spend time with him. His relationships were invariably short-term and sexual. For Steve, the prospect of a conquest was exhilarating, and he seemed to have little desire for a relationship beyond physical involvement. Many of his relationships were with women who he didn't, in fact, particularly like. His friends were amazed at his ability to have another girlfriend lined up whenever a relationship dissolved.

Inwardly, Steve often longed for a relationship that was more than just sexual. At times his feelings of loneliness were overwhelming. He periodically decided that with the next woman he would move slower, be less aggressive physically, but it never changed. He always followed the same pattern, and his relationships never lasted long. After becoming sexually involved with a woman, he soon found himself feeling closed in, and he wanted to escape.

At times it crossed Steve's mind that something might be wrong, but he quickly dismissed the thought. He rationalized his behavior by thinking that he was just naturally affectionate and had a very strong sex drive. The latter seemed to be confirmed by his need to masturbate in spite of a sexual relationship with his girlfriends.

When Steve met Ann, something seemed to change. He felt differently toward her than any of his previous girlfriends. Although he still enjoyed their sexual relationship, his desire to be with her was stronger than it had been for any other girl. After ten months of steady dating, Steve and Ann were married.

After the wedding Steve vowed to devote himself totally to Ann. After a few weeks, however, he began masturbating again. His job had become more stressful, and Steve used the stress to justify his need for "release," as he called it. Within six months of their marriage, Steve began secretly visiting adult bookstores and massage parlors. While he felt deeply guilty, he reminded himself of his strong sex drive and concluded that the most loving thing was not to burden Ann with it. Before long he was visiting prostitutes almost weekly.

After the birth of their son, Michael, Steve and Ann's sexual relationship slowed down for several months. Although their frequency of intercourse resumed before long, Steve spent two years justifying his compulsion by telling himself that he needed release and his wife wasn't available.

By this time Steve was living in two completely different worlds. One was a world of cheap motel rooms, adult bookstores, and dingy massage parlors. The other was a warm, loving family who wanted to be close to him. Steve was aware of his feeling of loneliness even while he was with his wife and son. While he was single, the dichotomy between his addiction and the rest of his life was not so great. He wasn't really close to anyone, and his addictive behavior was normalized and ignored by a permissive culture. His deep sense of isolation was hidden in sexual activity.

Steve had a natural ability to talk, and people naturally trusted him. This gift made him very successful at his sales job and helped him cover up his compulsive behavior. He soon found himself caught in a web of lies and deceitful excuses. He'd lie to his boss about sales meetings he'd missed because he was "cruising" for prostitutes. He'd lie to Ann about being late when he'd visited a porn shop. Once a client mentioned one of Steve's missed appointments to Ann, and they discovered that Steve had told each of them a different story regarding his whereabouts. Through a complex series of excuses, Steve was able to extricate himself from even that situation. By this time he'd become an accomplished liar. Steve was aware that he'd become compulsive in ways he didn't want to be. His big fear was that if anyone found out he'd be totally rejected and lose everything he valued.

Once, while shopping with Ann, Steve made a stop at a rest room specifically to masturbate. It was at this time that he began to recognize his sickness. He had an attractive, loving wife available to him, yet he chose to have sex with himself. This was the first crack in his shield of denial. Several times while contemplating his situation he wept in shame and regret. He promised himself he would stop, but soon became involved again, sometimes on the very same day as his resolution.

Steve read in the paper that the vice squad had raided a porn theater he frequented. He'd been there just two days before the raid, and the news sent a chill through him. He vowed never to attend another porn show. Within a month, however, he was back in that same theater.

The turning point came after a physical examination for work when he was diagnosed as having genital herpes. Ann was devastated. Steve told her that it must have resulted from one impulsive incident at a convention several months earlier. He promised it was a mistake that would never recur. Ann said she needed time to think, and she took Michael, their son, to the coast for a few days to sort things out. While there, she thought a great deal about the patterns in their marriage and about Steve's continual excuses. She made phone calls to several of Steve's friends and coworkers, and after putting some of the facts together, she concluded that Steve had been lying to her for a long time.

When Ann came home she presented Steve with an ultimatum: either he seek counseling or she would leave him. Steve was terrified of revealing his secret life, even to a counselor, but the cost of his compulsion was now too great. He agreed to therapy.

Steve spent two years in both individual and group therapy. During that time, he discovered that many people had his problem. With the help of his therapist, his new friends, and the support of his wife, Steve was able to see things very differently. He discovered a relationship with Jesus Christ that he never knew was possible. The strength he found there gave him courage to make changes. It was never easy and his healing is still in process. Now, Steve's secret life is more a sad memory than a terrifying fear.

In Steve's situation, he was willing to sacrifice everything for sexual satisfaction. He repeatedly risked job, marriage, family, friends, and self-respect. He continually promised himself that he would change, that it would never happen again. Yet he found himself telling more and more lies to cover up his behavior. At times he lost track of the real truth because of his many lies, and his life was often on the verge of disaster because of his behavior. He hurt very deeply and was intensely lonely. Although he was aware that his sexual activity increased his pain, he continued in it.

Dr. Patrick Carnes, in his book *Out of the Shadows*, describes the problem:

> The addict uses—or abuses rather—one of the most exciting moments in human experience: sex. Sexual arousal becomes intensified. The addict's mood is altered as he or she enters the obsessive trance. The metabolic responses are like a rush through the body as adrenaline speeds up the body's functioning. The heart pounds as the addict focuses on his search object. Risk, danger, and even violence are the ultimate escalators. One can always increase the dosage on intoxication. Preoccupation effectively buries the personal pain of remorse and regret. The addict does not always have to act. Often just thinking about it brings relief.
>
> The sexual addict's excitement-seeking parallels some other types of compulsive/obsessive addicts. In that sense, there is little difference between the voyeur waiting for hours by a window for ninety seconds of nudity and the compulsive gambler hunching on a long shot. What makes the sexual addict different is that he draws upon the human emotions generated by courtship and passion.[2]

The most frightening aspect of Steve's problem was that no one suspected. Not one of his friends or coworkers would have guessed that Steve led a secret life. He had become an expert at covering up.

Denial

A primary factor that allows an addict to continue an addiction is a defense mechanism called denial. Denial is more complex than just telling a lie. Denial is the individual's ability to distort reality until no one recognizes the problem, including the addict himself. Denial is accomplished in many ways. Rationalizing, justifying, and ignoring the problem become so habitual that the denial can look and feel like reality. The following is a list of common rationalizations used by sexual addicts to hide their problem, even from themselves:

- Everyone does it, just in different ways.
- If only my wife were more interested in sex.
- What he/she/they don't know won't hurt him/her/them.
- Anyone would do the same thing if they were in my situation.
- The pressure builds up and I need release.
- I couldn't stop myself, because of what she was doing.
- All women really want it, they just play games.
- After all, sex is man's strongest drive.
- Nobody's really getting hurt.

Because the addict sincerely believes his excuses, he becomes increasingly separated from reality. Usually an intense crisis, such as arrest or divorce, is necessary to shake the addict from this delusional system. When no one in the addict's life is either aware of the problem or concerned about it, or is courageous enough to initiate such a crisis, the problem usually escalates.

The addict becomes an incredibly effective manipulator, largely because he learns to believe his own lies. In Steve's case, Ann occasionally became suspicious. Sometimes when she phoned the office he would be gone for hours without explanation. Several times, the money he spent for gas would far exceed the amount they'd budgeted. When Ann confronted Steve, he would come up with an elaborate, detailed story. If she expressed any doubt at all, Steve would become angry. He convinced himself that she would doubt him even if he were honest; therefore, it was her problem.

He responded to her questioning by accusing her of something. When she would explain herself, Steve would compare his excuse with hers and accuse her of being paranoid. Since this had the ring of truth,

Ann would begin to feel off-track and end up apologizing. Steve would then be convinced that his wife had a problem.

With each step in this process, Steve felt increasingly mistreated and misjudged. His focus would shift from what was being said to what he felt, which distorted reality even further. Since he felt unjustly accused and he acted innocent, it followed that Ann was being unreasonable and therefore had the problem. Her apology became his proof.

Steve's case was typical in that he projected blame onto others. To be able to continue in the addiction, the addict must find ways, however delusional, to attribute his problems to others. When an addict loses his job due to coworkers' complaints, the excuse is that the boss didn't like him or that business was slow. When an addict contracts an STD, it's no big deal because "everyone gets it sometime." When a relationship breaks up because of his inappropriate sexual behavior, it's because "she couldn't handle the relationship."

In the same way, compulsive masturbation, pornography, prostitution, exhibitionism, and dozens of other dysfunctional preoccupations become rationalized as normal and healthy. The problem escalates until a crisis occurs that the addict cannot rationalize away.

The problem has been described well by recovering sexual addicts. The following description has been taken from a publication of Sexaholics Anonymous, an organization of support groups for recovering sexual addicts:

> Many of us felt inadequate, unworthy, alone, and afraid. Our insides never matched what we saw on the outsides of others.
>
> Early on, we came to feel disconnected—from parents, from peers, from ourselves. We tuned out with fantasy and masturbation. We plugged-in by drinking in the pictures, the images, and pursuing the objects of our fantasies. We lusted and wanted to be lusted after.
>
> We became true addicts: sex with self, promiscuity, adultery, dependency relationships, and more fantasy. We got it through the eyes; we bought it, we sold it, we traded it, we gave it away. We were addicted to the intrigue, the tease, the

forbidden. The only way we knew to be free of it was to do it. "Please connect with me and make me whole," we cried with outstretched arms. Lusting after the big fix, we gave away our power to others.

This produced guilt, self-hatred, remorse, emptiness, and pain, and we were driven ever inward, away from reality, away from love, lost inside ourselves.

Our habit made true intimacy impossible. We could never know real union with another because we were addicted to the unreal. We went for the "chemistry," the connection that had the magic, *because* it bypassed intimacy and true union. Fantasy corrupted the real; lust killed love.

First addicts, then love-cripples, we took from others to fill up what was lacking in ourselves. Conning ourselves time and again that the next one would save us, we were really losing our lives.[3]

Basic Misbeliefs

The root of the addictive system lies in a series of false beliefs that are held by the addict. These false assumptions drive him toward preoccupation with sex. Each misbelief reflects the addict's self-concept and leads him to a distortion of reality. The four misbeliefs are

1. I am basically a bad, unworthy person
2. No one would love me as I am
3. My needs will never be met by others
4. My most important need is sex

Each of these misbeliefs is rooted in the addict's early family life. These roots reach back into confused messages and lies about love, acceptance, and self-worth from parents, peers, and significant others. To discuss these roots is beyond the scope of this book. For our purposes, suffice it to say that basic self-condemnation and distrust of relationships begins the cycle of impaired thinking that promotes sexual addiction. The resulting compulsive behavior in turn strength-ens these misbeliefs. The process develops as follows:

The first misbelief, *I am basically a bad, unworthy person,* is the core of these individuals' self-concepts. They view themselves as inadequate and failures, and they expect defeat. Most of these people have developed a mask of appropriate behavior to hide their deep feelings of worthlessness. They go to great lengths to hide these feelings from others, due to their second misbelief.

No one would love me as I am. This misbelief isolates the addict. It becomes very important to hide fears and insecurities in order to avoid rejection and abandonment. Although addicts inwardly assume blame and guilt for anything that goes wrong (based on the first misbelief), they aren't free to take much blame or express remorse, fearing rejection. It, therefore, becomes impossible to be emotionally close to another person. They often portray an image of never being wrong or vulnerable in any way. This image further isolates them from close relationships.

The third misbelief, *my needs will never be met by others,* is the fuel for the addiction. Since the addict is convinced that he is unlovable, it naturally follows that his needs for nurturance, acceptance, and love will not be met by others. He must therefore meet these needs alone. He cannot be relaxed and trusting in a relationship since he is totally responsible for his own nurturance. Consequently, he becomes manipulative and controlling. The irony is that he must appear unselfish, moral, and benevolent in order to avoid rejection. At the same time he must selfishly manipulate people into meeting his needs. The addict becomes the master of the double life. What he experiences internally and what he expresses externally become increasingly incongruent. His fear of discovery develops into a growing paranoia.

The fourth misbelief, *my most important need is sex,* serves to focus the tension that is caused by the other misbeliefs in the direction of sexual expression. In childhood the addict began a search for something to relieve the pain of unfulfilled emotional needs. Sexual sensations were discovered as something within his control that temporarily soothed emotional pain. In this way love, acceptance, and nurturance became translated into sex. The sexual addict is extremely afraid of living without sex since that would mean living without love and care. Since he is solely responsible for getting this need met, he is obsessed with sex.

The outcome of these false beliefs is addiction. The first three misbeliefs result in negative feelings of despair and loss of control. When an addict behaves sexually in some way, he receives a pleasant sensation (release) followed by feelings of intense shame. This shame reinforces the first three misbeliefs and drives the addict toward further sexual behavior. The addict says, "If the things I believe about myself are true, I can't change." The last misbelief gives a feeling of control, in that he feels he can control the meeting of his sexual need. Masturbation, sexual relationships, and visiting prostitutes are methods of control, all of which the addict feels guilty about.

A paradox emerges. Sexual activity never actually meets these needs but the addict believes it does. The result is an intensification and acceleration of the sexual behaviors that presumably will meet these needs. This intensification can be divided into three levels of sexual behaviors.

Levels of Addictive Behavior

It is important to understand that the behaviors discussed here are not automatically an indication of sexual addiction. Inappropriate sexual behavior is not necessarily an addiction. Some people practice sexual behaviors that they regret and yet continue. These people are not necessarily addicts. The addict is a person whose life is out of control because of *constant preoccupation* with sexual activity. The addict is not simply a person with a sexual problem; he is a person with a sexual *obsession*.

It is important to note, too, that addiction at one of the following levels does not necessarily predict a progression to the next level. Some addicts practice only level 1 behaviors and never progress to more serious activities. The commonality among addicts is that the behavior is compulsive and out of control. The sexual behavior has become the focus of the addict's daily routine, despite any risks involved. Many marriages, families, and even lives have been ruined by compulsive level 1 behavior.

While a person addicted at level 1 may never progress to level 2 or 3, it's very doubtful that the opposite is true. An addict at level 2 or 3 inevitably was compulsive at level 1. In this sense the levels represent a progression.

Level 1 behaviors are either not classified as illegal, or are referred to as victimless crimes. Our society has decided that they are tolerable, and in some sectors, even normal. They are behaviors that easily become compulsive and are the foundations of the sexual crimes of levels 2 and 3. Level 1 behaviors include compulsive masturbation, prostitution, pornography, homosexuality, and extramarital affairs. Level 1 behaviors may also include heterosexual relationships that are compulsively sexual in nature. Chronic selfish sexual demands that are distasteful or insensitive to the partner may also be included at level 1. In general, an addict is not limited to any one particular behavior, but is involved in many.

Level 2 behaviors are clearly illegal and involve a victim. The possible consequences of getting caught become part of the excitement of sexual arousal. Although our legal system forbids these activities, our society generally views the offenders with pity. They are seen as a nuisance rather than a threat, and the legal penalties are relatively minor. While there are clearly victims of these crimes, there is no physical harm inflicted. These behaviors include exhibitionism, voyeurism, obscene phone calls, and indecent liberties—touching another person in an intimate manner without his or her consent.

Level 3 behaviors are serious crimes. Damage and injury to the victim is significant. Although leniency may be practiced within the legal system in some of these cases, such is certainly not the accepted attitude. In general, our society has little patience for offenders in this category. They commit significant crimes with profound consequences, including child molestation, incest, rape, and violence.

Recognizing Early stages

How can an individual recognize sexual compulsivity as it is developing? The difficulty is that so much of the compulsion is internal. The addicted individual must be honest with himself and fight off the tendency toward denial. An individual who can do so has the potential to deal with sexual compulsion before it reaches an addictive stage; many people cannot. The following are guidelines for self-evaluating compulsive behavior:

1. Sexual behavior is used to change one's mood rather than to express intimate affection. When the purpose of sex is to avoid negative feelings, or when it becomes a source of painful feelings, it is a sign of the addictive process.
2. The sexual behavior creates pain or problems for the individual or others. Degrading oneself or exploiting others is a symptom of sexual addiction.
3. The behavior has to be kept secret. Behavior that cannot be shared with another individual indicates guilt and shame and leads to a double life.
4. The relationships involved are devoid of commitment. This is because the addict uses sex to avoid a genuine relationship.

The above are warning signs, and they indicate escalating sexual compulsivity. They are helpful only to the individual who is willing to be painfully honest with himself.

Is My partner an Addict?

This question is a valid one and deserves some straight answers. What follows are some signals that could indicate an addiction or a dangerous obsession. None of these warning signs should be taken lightly.

When you continually feel sexually taken advantage of by your partner, these feelings, regardless of how either of you justify them, are a danger signal. They indicate an imbalance in the relationship. Realizing that you are compromising your own values or are sacrificing important parts of the relationship for the sake of your partner's sexual satisfaction is another important signal. It indicates that the relationship is one-sided and that sex is the primary focus.

It is important to share these feelings of being used or being taken advantage of with your partner. If your partner minimizes or discounts your feelings, it's an indication that your emotional needs are seen as insignificant compared to your partner's physical needs. At this point it becomes clear that your partner is remaining in the relationship in exchange for sex. Significant changes need to be made in order to have a healthy relationship.

Other warning signs include chronic lies about relationships or questionable behavior, constant justification or rationalization of inappropriate sexual behavior, activities that always seem to be directed toward sexually compromising or seductive situations.

All of these signals are indicative of a sexual addiction. If these signals are present, with or without actual addiction, they are clear signs of a very unhealthy relationship.

Is There Hope?

As bleak and despairing as this picture may seem, there is hope for the sexual addict. There is forgiveness and healing in a union with God at the cross. There are caring people who are available to help. There are also sexual addicts who have overcome their compulsion and want to share their victory with others who suffer. But the individual addict must take the first step, and that is where the primary difficulty lies.

Denial, rationalization, and secrecy are an intricate part of this disorder. It's a sad fact that most addicts will not understand the depth of their problem until life falls apart. Arrest, divorce, abandonment, injury, and job loss are crises that motivate an addict to search for recovery.

There is an irony in the close relationships of the addict. Those closest to the addict often do the most harm in their attempt to help. The spouse, parents, and friends unwittingly protect the addict from disaster. They often justify, excuse, deny, and lie for the addict in order to protect him from the consequences of his behavior. They may choose not to confront inappropriate behavior. They repeatedly accept shaky excuses for irresponsible actions and broken commitments. They provide alibis to employers, children, and others who experience the consequences of the addict's behavior. By preventing a crisis they take away the main motivation for change. This only perpetuates the problem by helping the addict hold on to an illusion of normalcy. Until the addict can feel the full impact of his actions, chances are slim that he'll seek help. Removing the protective support is the most difficult yet important action a loved one can take.

The first step toward recovery is for the addict to admit his helplessness and then to seek help. The recovery process for the addict revolves around acknowledging and understanding the four basic misbeliefs mentioned earlier that destroy reality. Feelings of worthlessness and abandonment need to be explored. Fear of trust and vulnerability needs to be resolved so that healthy relationships can be established. False beliefs must be replaced by healthy, realistic ones. New patterns of relating to others must be learned. All of this cannot be accomplished by the addict alone. His recovery will depend upon support from others.

Essential to the recovery of the sexual addict is participation in a support group. The addict must commit himself to those who are interested in growth and recovery; in such a group there can be mutual support and empathy while each person is held accountable for his own behavior. These groups are based on an adaptation of the "Twelve Steps" of Alcoholics Anonymous and have been developing for several decades in the United States, Europe, and Canada.

Through these twelve steps the individual comes to acknowledge that the problem is more powerful than he is. He has become powerless over his addiction to lust. He must develop a faith in and dependence upon God to overcome his compulsion. The source of the addict's life and self-worth must be God, rather than the addiction.

He must develop healthy, trusting relationship patterns within the group context and take responsibility for past, present, and future actions. The process is slow and painful, but the results are positive.

When an individual is willing to seek help for his compulsion, many resources are available. There are professionals who specialize in working with compulsive behavior, and there are many support groups that focus on resolving sexual addiction.

At this point the literature available on sexual addiction is growing rapidly. Material is available through Sexaholics Anonymous. For literature and information concerning support groups in your area, you may write to Sexaholics Anonymous headquarters:

> S.A.
> P.O. Box 300
> Simi Valley, CA 93062

Other recommended books:

- *God, Help Me Stop* by Claire W. An independently published workbook for compulsive behaviors.[4]
- *The Twelve Steps for Everyone* by Grateful Members.[5]

The following test was developed by Sexaholics Anonymous to help an individual evaluate his or her tendency toward sexual addiction.

1. Have you ever thought you needed help for your sexual thinking or behavior?
2. Have you thought that you'd be better off if you didn't keep "giving in"?
3. Have you thought that sex or sexual stimuli are controlling you?
4. Have you ever tried to stop or limit doing what you felt was wrong in your sexual behavior?
5. Do you resort to sex to escape, relieve anxiety, or because you can't cope?
6. Do you feel guilt, remorse, or depression afterward?

7. Has your pursuit of sex become more compulsive?
8. Does it interfere with relations with your spouse?
9. Do you have to resort to images or memories during sex?
10. Does an irresistible impulse arise when the other party makes the overture or sex is offered?
11. Do you keep going from one "relationship" or lover to another?
12. Do you feel the "right relationship" would help you stop lusting, masturbating, or being so promiscuous?
13. Do you have a destructive need—a desperate sexual or emotional need for someone?
14. Does pursuit of sex make you careless for yourself or the welfare of your family or others?
15. Has your effectiveness or concentration decreased as sex has become more compulsive?
16. Do you lose time from work because of it?
17. Do you turn to a lower environment when pursuing sex?
18. Do you want to get away from the sex partner as soon as possible after the act?
19. Although your spouse is sexually compatible, do you still masturbate or have sex with others?
20. Have you ever been arrested for a sex-related offense?[6]

Karlyn's Thoughts
Overwhelming Infection

H ave you ever had athlete's foot? I haven't, but my dad and my boyfriend had a tag-team discussion the other day to explain it to me. It sounds absolutely disgusting.

It starts out as a sharp itch between your toes. My boyfriend described it as "not a normal itch—it's kind of sharp and stinging, and it feels like something deeper than just a mosquito bite." You can't see anything there, and it just takes a quick rub to make it go away. But it comes back five minutes later and you have to rub it away again.

Soon it takes more of a pinch to ease the itch, and it starts to come back more often. The skin gets redder, and little hivelike bumps appear. It starts to spread. You can't relieve it anymore by just rubbing at it; now you have to scratch and rip at it with your fingernails. Then you find something else, something harder—a pen cap or a stick—to scrape at it with. But the itch only gets worse. You take a terrycloth towel and pull it back and forth between your toes to relieve the torment. When you stop, for a second you think it's gone, but then it comes back even worse. Pretty soon it won't go away at all; you get no relief.

It practically takes over your life. You can't go *anywhere* without trying to scratch it. You'll trip yourself trying to scratch one foot with the other while you're walking. You know that if you don't leave it alone it's only going to get worse, and you try to steel yourself against the onslaught, but you always cave. You *have* to scratch it. You know that you'll never get rid of it by tearing at it, and that you're only making it worse, but you don't know what else to do. It doesn't take long before you've scratched it so much that it breaks open and bleeds— but *still* that incessant stinging itch is there. Your constant scratching is only an *illusion* of relief; it never makes the bacteria go away. The only way to get rid of athlete's foot is to go to your doctor and get a prescription cream; and even then, especially if it's open and bleeding, it's going to hurt. And it will take a *long* time to heal. Athlete's foot is a pain.

So is having a sexual addiction. It starts out as nothing much—a lingering look at a lingerie ad, maybe—but it gets steadily worse. Fantasies get more and more descriptive as you get more "educated" and your imagination is fired up. Real faces start appearing in your fantasies. Pretty soon you're never free of the burning desire for relief; it's a pressure, a tension, that *has* to be placated, but nothing seems to satisfy the craving.

I can relate to having overwhelming sexual feelings, and when I think about having them all day, every day, my energy level plummets.

It would be so draining, so taxing on a body to be desperately hungry for pleasure *all the time.* The need to be healed and actually fulfilled would be superseded only by the embarrassment of needing to be healed in the first place. I understand that feeling of shame.

I used to think I hadn't experienced sexual addiction. Even as I wrote the first draft for this chapter, I didn't know what I was going to say because I didn't think it applied to me. But God has shown me how much I *have* struggled with sexual addiction. Perhaps not as harshly as many, but the infection is still there. Lust and fantasies are just as real in a woman's world as in a man's, and it's a heavy burden for all of us. If we really want to be free of such a constant burden, go to the Doctor. Jesus has the prescription you need. Put that cream on your sores and grit your teeth as it starts to heal. Find trusted friends to hold your hand and support you because it's *not* going to be easy; the bacteria are burrowed down deep. The addiction can be eradicated, but you've got to be willing to spend the time. You've got to *want* to be free of the pain.

I've seen friends attacked with a sexual addiction. Unless you know them well you can't tell anything's wrong, but if you start to get deeper you'll see the blood trickling out of the sores every once in a while. If you really dig and find out what's going on, you'll see that it's taking over their lives—it's an obsession that controls them and everything they do. It's one of the worst things I've ever watched happen to a human being.

Don't allow nasty, itching bacteria to steal your life away. Jesus has more power than any addiction will *ever* hold over you! Stop scratching and fight back.

7

The other side of the coin

Bob and Jane had been married three weeks when they first came to see me. Jane was extremely depressed. Bob was frustrated. Both expressed disillusionment with their sexual relationship.

"When we were dating, we did everything right," said Bob, almost angrily. "We prayed, we read the Bible, we talked a lot, we never had sex, we followed all the rules. In spite of all that, our wedding night was an absolute disaster. We both felt that somehow everything was wrong. She was scared, and I was uncomfortable. Afterward, we both felt awful—kind of guilty and kind of angry. It's gotten a little better since then, but not much. We both feel betrayed; no one told us it would be like this."

The three of us spent some time discussing a number of specifics about their courtship. Their approach to sexuality was the opposite extreme of most couples I've talked with. Their sexual commitment to each other was to have their first kiss on the wedding night. They had decided to avoid all physical contact until their vows were formalized in marriage.

Total Abstinence Before Marriage

I've encountered a number of engaged couples who have approached their sexual involvement from this perspective. Like Bob and Jane, they are usually committed, well-intentioned, and fairly self-disciplined Christians.

Their logic makes sense. "If we're going to spend our lives together, there'll be plenty of time for sex. If we aren't going to get married, why get started?"

I won't debate the logic behind Bob and Jane's decision. If a couple decides to handle their physical relationship this way, I strongly encourage them to maintain their convictions. There are, however, some hazards to this approach.

Strong warnings against sexual promiscuity may give the impression that the opposite must necessarily be true—if uncontrolled sexual liberty is bad, total physical abstinence must be great. If we take this reasoning to its logical conclusion, the ideal lifestyle would be that of a priest or monk—committed to celibacy for life, involved only in purely spiritual pursuits.

Sometimes this seems like the only reasonable alternative to physical intimacy. And that's what the disciples suggested to Jesus when he explained the significance of divorce to them in Matthew 19. His response was interesting. He pointed out that not everyone could handle the single lifestyle but "only those to whom it has been given" (v. 11). The implication is that for most of us, celibacy is probably not the solution. Somewhere there must be a balanced course of healthy sexual development and expression for individuals as well as couples.

Remember that sexual desire and involvement follow a natural progression in a relationship. Let's say that, for the couple planning to marry, the progression begins with holding hands and ends with sexual intercourse after the wedding. The process is, of course, much more complex than that, but to illustrate it in graph form would look like this:

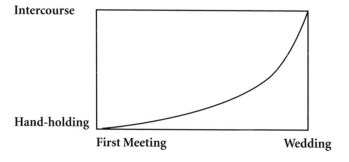

From the time a couple begins a relationship until the time of their marriage, sexual progression struggles for physical expression. (The implications of that expression happening too early in the relationship have been thoroughly discussed earlier in this book.) If we assume that the couple's goal is to eventually marry (which is not always the case) then for those couples, whose physical involvement progresses so quickly that intercourse occurs before the wedding, the graph may look like this. Here's where so many patterns of sexual problems have their start.

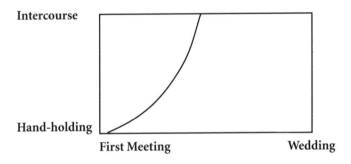

Intercourse

Hand-holding

First Meeting   **Wedding**

For a couple who's decided to abstain from the expression of physical affection, like Bob and Jane, the graph would look like this:

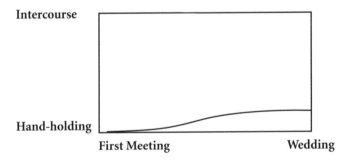

Intercourse

Hand-holding

First Meeting   **Wedding**

Here the concept of premature consummation is introduced. Premature consummation refers to the difference between the emotional development of a couple's physical relationship and their expectations for intercourse. In other words, a couple may not be emotionally ready for intercourse even though they have just been married. I need to emphasize that premature consummation is not a legal or moral issue; it is an emotional one. Premature consummation takes place when emotional development has been short-circuited.

problems with premature consummation

As previously stated, sexual involvement is progressive. It is also a fact that our biological and emotional functions aren't always controlled by logical reasoning. Since these two things are true, it may be unrealistic to assume that something (premarital sex) that has been treated as absolutely taboo for years can automatically be turned 180 degrees and experienced as absolutely wonderful a few hours after the wedding. Our minds may say yes, but chances are good that our emotions will say no. Young couples may experience guilt and fear even when there is nothing to feel guilty or fearful about. While there is nothing legal, moral, or scriptural to base these emotions upon, the feelings are experienced just the same. The natural process of bonding needs to be recognized and respected. Shortcutting the process results in emotional and relational problems.

Additional factors can make the wedding night less than enjoyable for couples like Bob and Jane. For example, the first intercourse is often painful for the woman. That pain, coupled with the tension and apprehension of such a major switch in perspective, response, and behavior, can make for a very negative experience. It's also possible that the new husband may be unaware of his bride's needs and desires. He may have trouble controlling how soon he comes to climax himself. All of these factors complicated Bob and Jane's experience, and started their sexual relationship with a load of negative emotions.

Delayed consummation

If you mutually choose to avoid all physical involvement prior to marriage, please don't let anyone convince you that you must have intercourse on your wedding night. I know many couples who would have developed a healthier and happier sexual relationship if they had not been in such a hurry to consummate their union on the wedding night. Weariness, frustration, tension, fear, ignorance—all have the potential to make the experience a miserable one.

Here are some suggestions to help you sidestep some of these potential problems. Begin by having a discussion shortly before your wedding day. Talk openly and honestly about what would be most comfortable for each of you. The discussion may feel awkward at first, but it will save you years of regret and painful memories. Following this discussion, set your limits according to the more modest of the two of you. This means if the husband feels comfortable caressing his wife's body but she feels comfortable with only kissing, agree to go no further than kissing for now. Allow her to become comfortable with the progression at her own pace. It is perfectly acceptable to move through the stages of kissing, French kissing, petting, and fondling before intercourse during the days and weeks after the wedding.

If you move through the stages as they feel comfortable, you'll enjoy complete sexual intimacy much more than you would have on your wedding night. In terms of your sexual expression graph, the progression would look like this:

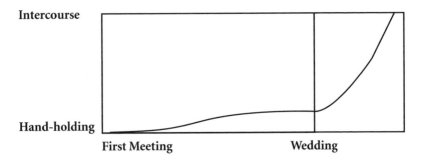

In his book, *Solomon on Sex*, Joseph Dillow gives an excellent suggestion for couples like Bob and Jane who prefer to move more slowly and modestly in their sexual relationship:

Let the new bride get into the bath first while the husband is in the other room. A candle lit in the bathroom, being the only light, will produce a warm, romantic atmosphere. As they relax together in the bathtub, they can discuss the day, talk and even pray thanking the Lord for the gift of each other. As they communicate and share, the warm water drains away the tensions of the day and the bubbles sufficiently hide the wife's body so she is not immediately embarrassed. They should then begin to gently stimulate each other under the water, hidden by the bubble bath. As the sexual tension and anticipation mounts, many of the initial inhibitions begin to melt away and a transfer to the bedroom is more natural.[1]

There are many other ways to overcome inhibition, but the most important elements are these: relax, talk openly about your feelings, and let things progress at the rate that is most comfortable for both of you. Make it an adventure of discovering each other. Be ready to laugh at yourselves and with one another when things don't go as smoothly as they do in the movies (because they almost never do). It will give you stories to laugh about for years, although you may never get to tell them to anyone else.

Misunderstanding god's view of sex

For some couples, sexual abstinence is not the result of a mutual decision. Rather, it is frequently the result of ignorance, misbelief, and a misunderstanding of God's intention for married love. Such was the case with Tim and Judy.

Both Tim and Judy came from families with strict moral standards. Both families were missionaries in northern Africa, where Tim and Judy met as children. Neither considered their families affectionate—hugs and kisses were seldom exchanged between family members. Tim could not remember the topic of sex ever being mentioned at home. The only discussion of sex that Judy had been exposed to while growing up revolved around the dangerous sins of lust and fornication.

When Tim and Judy came back to the United States to attend Bible college, each found very few friends who shared their conservative views. So they were naturally attracted to each other and were married shortly after graduation.

When they made an appointment for counseling they had been married for almost a year. During our first session it became clear that they had not yet experienced sexual intercourse. Tim felt frustrated and vaguely guilty about his sexual desire toward his bride. Whenever he brought up the subject, Judy reminded him that they were not yet ready to have children and made comments questioning his spirituality. Tim had stopped bringing up the topic, but was bothered by lustful thoughts, guilt, and resentment.

In several sessions I carefully showed Tim and Judy how God views sex in marriage, and they eventually realized that they needed to work on revamping their views about sex to coincide with Scripture.

Tim and Judy had projected their own ideas onto God. They had become familiar with bits and pieces of Scripture that supported the message they assumed to be there.

Some well-meaning Christians teach that the sex act is a result of Adam's sin. They believe that when Adam brought sin to the human race by eating forbidden fruit, part of that sin was sexual intercourse. Take a look at the first chapter of the book of Genesis. Read the whole chapter, then focus on verse 28:

> God blessed them and said to them, "Be fruitful and increase in number; fill the earth and subdue it. Rule over the fish of the sea and the birds of the air and over every living creature that moves on the ground."

God is telling Adam and Eve to increase in number, and that means sex. Unless God had made some significant changes in human anatomy that He didn't tell us about, sex for Adam and Eve was basically the same as it is for us today.

The sin of Adam and the subsequent fall of man doesn't occur until the third chapter of Genesis. This tells us that God created and ordained the sex act before sin entered the world. So much for sex being inherently bad. Now take a look at verse 31:

> God saw all that he had made, and it was very good. And there was evening, and there was morning—the sixth day.

When God says that everything He made was very good, He's including sex in the package, as well as all of man's and woman's anatomy. This has some interesting implications. One part of the female anatomy is a small organ called the clitoris. It is located just above the vagina. The clitoris has a large number of nerve endings and is extremely responsive to touch. It's interesting that the clitoris has no discernible function except for physical stimulation and arousal. This indicates that the clitoris was created by God with no other purpose than sexual pleasure. That tells us quite a bit about God's view of sex.

Think about it—after creating the sex act, after creating all parts of human sexual anatomy, "God saw all that he had made, and it was very good." If you read Genesis 2:25, you'll see that Adam and Eve felt good about it, too. God always intended for sex to be good, clean fun.

The Bible promotes and encourages sex within the stability of a marriage commitment, never outside of it. Within the loving marriage commitment God gives no restrictions at all.

This is difficult for many Christians to accept because their sexual drives seem to be condemned by Paul's statements about "the lusts of the flesh." Many Christians actually manufacture restrictions that seem godly to them. In reality, most only serve to limit fulfillment. In chapter 9 we'll take a closer look at what God has said about sexuality.

Tim and Judy began to discover the positive side of God's gift of sex through their own study of the Bible. They began to understand and experience the exciting freedom of the physical love God intended for married couples. For them, marriage became an exciting adventure they never knew was possible.

Growing closer

1. If you were to choose to avoid any physical involvement prior to marriage, how would your friends react? How would your family respond? How do you usually respond to peer pressure: compromise, withdrawal, or consistency? How do you think your decision would be affected by your friends' and/or family members' reactions?
2. If you've made a decision to delay physical involvement, how do you believe your past relationships have affected this decision?
3. For a more thorough treatment of the subject, you may want to read

   • *Romantic Lovers* by David Hocking[2]
   • *Solomon on Sex* by Joseph Dillow[3]

Karlyn's Thoughts
Slow and Steady Wins the Race

If there's one thing I've learned in the dating game, it's that everything is about *balance*. I remember when I was sixteen (sweet and never been kissed). I read a book in which one of the characters had promised not to kiss anyone until he and his bride were at the altar. I thought that was cool, so I decided I wanted to do that too. I wrote a letter to my future husband telling him of my decision, sealed it, dated it, and shoved it into a drawer to keep until that wonderful day.

Then, as I got older—and the prospect of serious dating got closer—I decided it might be a good idea to lighten up a bit, so I changed my promise to save my first kiss until engagement. That seemed a little more reasonable.

Enter: guys.

Enter: issues.

Over the next few years—through my first romantic relationship and into college where my first serious relationship began—that boundary kept getting pushed back. I *did* stay firmly at waiting until engagement through that first relationship. In between the two relationships, though, the boundary got moved so that I could kiss someone when I just *knew* I was going to marry him—*before* it was actually official. Then at nineteen, when I started dating my first serious boyfriend, I struggled for months over changing it yet again. I didn't want to pressure myself into caving just because I wanted to, but at the same time I felt like my no-kissing rule *had* been useful at one time, but was now impractical—and completely agonizing. I thought and prayed hard about it. I finally decided it was time to change the boundary line again: this time, my first kiss would be with a man I was truly in love with. My boyfriend and I talked about what being in love meant, and I asked him to kiss me only when he knew *he* was in love with *me*. Not too long after that I got my long-awaited first kiss. And I haven't regretted my decision.

My point is, we often walk a fine line as we try to find healthy boundaries. I had to find balance in my decision to kiss: what was right to stay away from versus what was right to do so that temptation wouldn't have a foothold. It's a battle that surrounds every physical boundary. That fine line is going to fall in different places for different people, simply because temptation in certain areas is greater for some people than for others. To clarify, however, I'm *not* suggesting that for some people it might be okay to have sex. Sleeping with someone throws everything out of balance; I've seen moving *that* boundary played out unhappily in too many of my friends' lives. Because God created sex as a sealing of the union between a man and his wife, when you enjoy it prematurely you *join* yourself to that person for the *rest of your life.* "For this reason a man will leave his father and mother and be united to his wife, and *the two will become one flesh*" (Eph. 5:31). If you decide to break up, you'll always be missing a part of you. That's not balance. That's tipping the scales.

There *is* one thing that's the same for every couple, no matter what their boundaries: wherever you draw your line, you'll be tempted to cross it. Sometimes it *is* the right time to extend certain boundaries (like my kissing rule that kept changing as I went through different stages of my life). But other times we need to stick it out and ask for God's strength to beat the temptation. It can be *so* hard to tell the difference between when to be flexible and when not to be. Here's a key word that I've found to be the answer in practically 100 percent of my physical boundary issues—*wait*.

Let's say I'm in the heat of the moment one night and I desperately want to cross a boundary. If I wait until at least the next morning (a couple of days is even better), I can see a lot more clearly whether I'm really supposed to move that boundary. Besides, that gives me time to consult God on the issue. The desire to have more than we're getting will always be there; and since all these desires aren't going away, we have to figure out how to set our boundaries based on what God has planned for our sexual safety.

Admittedly, doing so can get a little difficult. First of all, besides "no sex outside of marriage," He's not very clear on the specifics of physical boundaries. He doesn't say, "Thou shalt not French kiss until thou hast been dating for one year and then a fortnight . . . ," but He *does* talk about keeping your mind pure. "Fix your thoughts on what is true and honorable and right. Think about things that are pure and lovely and admirable. Think about things that are excellent and worthy of praise" (Phil. 4:8–9 NLT).

Okay, there's my boundary. If I can't pray while I'm doing it, I shouldn't be doing it. The healthy balance in setting your boundaries comes from looking ahead, knowing yourself and your limits, and setting boundaries that are realistic for *you*. Don't make boundaries that are so restricting that you feel like a martyr half the time. That's not a healthy balance either. Say when you first started dating you were only comfortable with side hugs. Now it's been four months and you want to wrap her in your arms and hold her every now and then, but you're afraid that moving boundaries would be sinful. Don't be afraid to talk together and decide as a *team* to move the boundary

back. Don't refuse to move it simply because you think you're supposed to suffer through these "sinful" desires that make you want to
be close to each other.

What would have happened if I'd stuck to the idea I'd had at sixteen years old and kept my first kiss until my wedding day? Since I'll
never actually be in that position, I can't know for sure. What I *do*
know is that right now I'd be having a very tough time with the pressure of desiring something I wouldn't let myself have. The thing is, *I
could handle kissing.* I *can* pray and thank God while I'm kissing my
boyfriend. To stay where I was at sixteen would have been me being
scared of letting God control the timing. My point is, sometimes you
might have great intentions in keeping your physical involvement
nearly nonexistent while dating, but it's not always a sinful compromise to reevaluate your boundaries—especially when holding back
gets to be ridiculously hard.

When you're working as a team to keep each other pure and you're
following what God tells you to do, your boundaries will keep a healthy
balance. Sometimes that might mean your relationship is very hands-
off: that's okay, but please don't expect yourselves to fall passionately
into each other's arms after the wedding. A wedding is a ceremony; it
doesn't do anything to change your mind or your heart. If you've had
a very conservative courtship, it's okay to keep dating each other after
marriage and *build up to* finally sleeping together—don't put a timeline
on it. There's no rush.

As you're trying to figure out where your boundaries should lie,
keep in mind the criteria Christ has set up for you already: "For you
remember what we taught you in the name of the Lord Jesus. God
wants you to be holy, so you should keep clear of all sexual sin. Then
each of you will control your body and live in holiness and honor—
not in lustful passion as the pagans do, in their ignorance of God and
his ways" (1 Thess. 4:2–5 NLT).

8

Discovering Freedom

So far, in talking about sexual promiscuity, we've discussed the whys and wherefores, the sociological and psychological problems, and the theological implications. When all is said and done, however, we have to get back to the question of how we make remaining sexually pure practical. What can a couple do today that will get them back on the right track or keep problems from beginning?

Our society, especially the media—movies, television, music, magazines, books—constantly pumps us full of sexually arousing material. We can't watch an evening of TV or thumb through a magazine without being confronted with sexual messages in a hundred different ways. It's difficult *not* to get preoccupied with sex. The message we receive is that sexual liberties without commitment are no big deal. Traditional, biblical values are nonsense. Sex is considered casual, recreational, and without moral implication one way or another. Besides, sex feels good. The sensation of arousal is pleasant, so our bodies propel us toward the very actions that cause such deep and complex problems.

Contrary to popular belief, we do not have to be driven to action by these impulses. They may be natural and normal, but it's a myth that they are overpowering or irresistible. We choose how we allow them to affect us, and we choose our behavior in response to them. I once heard Dr. Sol Gorden give an excellent illustration of this capacity. Picture two teenagers on the couch, passionately making out and getting more and more intense. At one point the boy says, "I've got to go for it. I can't help myself. There's no stopping it." The girl only needs to say, "I think I hear my mother coming," and that young man will suddenly find a way to stop. It's amazing.

As the Christian single develops a standard of sexual expression, the issues discussed in this book become extremely relevant. It's clear that Scripture says chastity is a requisite of Christian singleness, and that the consequences of disobedience can be severe. God has not only given us the responsibility of living within these limits, He created us with the ability to do so. For the sincere individual or couple who wants their physical relationship to progress in a biblical, healthy, realistic way, there is a great deal of hope.

Preparing for a lifetime commitment is an extensive process. It takes much time and effort. Unfortunately, most people spend more time preparing to get a driver's license than preparing for marriage. The following suggestions regarding sexual development are applicable to any couple who want to maintain or regain sexual purity.

1. *If you've been sexually active as a couple, agree that it's a problem and that it will damage your relationship.* Regardless of the justification for the sexual relationship, it's important that each of you asks forgiveness of one another and of God. By verbalizing your regrets and mistakes, this particular conversation becomes a marker for the turning point of your relationship. It will also help you become accountable to one another for the development of your relationship. Commit yourselves to making a change in this area.

2. *Avoid sexually stimulating material.* This includes pornographic films or literature and openly suggestive television programs or music. Beware of anything that artificially stimulates desire. These examples may seem innocent or even trite, but exposing yourself to their influence lowers motivation to remain pure and leads to compromising of values. By staying away from

stimulation as individuals, couples will find it much easier to avoid temptation as a unit.

3. *Spend time in material that is positive and strengthens biblical values.* There's no substitute for reading and meditating on Scripture. Countless good books and cassette tapes are available that can replace the negative sexual input we encounter daily. You may have some favorite inspirational speakers or writers. If not, your pastor or local Christian bookstore may have some suggestions.

   A saying among computer programmers is true for everyone: "Garbage in . . . garbage out." We can choose what we allow to fill our minds, and what our minds are filled with will control our behavior. "For as [a man] thinks within himself, so he is" (Proverbs 23:7 NASB).

4. *Avoid purposely or consciously escalating sexual arousal in one another.* Ask the question, "Can I morally satisfy the desires I'm arousing in this person?" If you cannot (and you cannot if you are not married to that person), then the arousal of your partner's passion is a type of defrauding. The normal, healthy emotional development of the loving relationship you really desire is stifled, and the traps discussed throughout this book are being baited and set.

5. *Sit down together and honestly discuss your beliefs, hopes, and fears, as well as your desires regarding your physical relationship.* Be specific as you talk about what puts each of you in the danger zone. This will take a great deal of honesty and vulnerability. You cannot control sexual urges by denying them. You will need to discuss them and develop a plan. Don't pretend you don't enjoy sex if you do enjoy it. Admit the potential for serious problems and make some mutual decisions about handling temptation. Your ability and willingness to communicate on this level will tell you a great deal about your readiness for marriage. If you or your partner cannot or will not do this, it's a signal that the relationship needs a great deal of development before marriage. By discussing it as a couple, you both

take responsibility for this part of the relationship. Neither partner should get away with saying, "You stop me." Only a team effort will strengthen intimacy and communication.

6. *Decide together on a level of physical involvement that promotes and develops genuine communication in the relationship.* Go with the more conservative view. This means if you're comfortable with long periods of kissing in a parked car, and your partner prefers no more than a good-night kiss on the porch, the limit should be a good-night kiss on the porch. Otherwise, there still will be the struggle with guilt and the potential for developing illicitness. One of you may feel used by the other and start resenting it. Beware of a partner who attempts to coerce you into deeper levels of involvement that make you uncomfortable. The concern may be more for self-gratification than for developing a healthy, mutually satisfying relationship. In this case, marriage plans are probably premature.

7. *Discuss whether there may be certain times, places, or situations that predictably lead one or both of you into temptation in this area.* You may discover that either or both of you are more easily tempted being in a parked car at night or lying on the couch together. It's important that you both know your areas of temptation and discuss them together as specifically as possible. Exploring these specifics together will help you find and agree upon the limits of your physical relationship. Doing so will require honest communication and creativity, skills that are essential in a healthy marriage. The following are examples from my case files of specific limits different couples have agreed upon.

• *No kissing unless we're standing up.* This couple decided that temptation became too strong when they sat or laid down while kissing.
• *No physical contact after 10 p.m.* This couple discovered that temptation was greatest late at night when they were tired and their motivation to resist was low.

• *No removal of any clothing.* This couple felt comfortable with the agreement that the first button, zipper, or snap that was undone or opened signaled that the boundaries had been crossed, and they needed to separate for a while.

• *Stay off the couch when we're alone.* This couple found that the couch in either of their apartments was the place of greatest temptation, so they decided to sit elsewhere when they were alone together.

Set the boundaries early enough in the arousal process so that you both agree it is realistic to stop. If your plan is to get as involved and excited as you possibly can and then back off at the last minute, you're probably being unrealistic and will end up with regrets. It's important that you establish your goals and priorities *before* you are tempted. The time to look for a bomb shelter is before the enemy attacks.

The importance of taking these steps as a couple is illustrated by Dr. Dwight Carlson.

> It's like driving 90 mph down a city street and a child runs out in front of the car. We may jam on the brakes and have every intention of stopping, but the actual decision was made when we decided to go 90 mph on a city street. Once that decision is made, it's sometimes very difficult to reverse.
>
> The same holds true in sexual temptation: The amount of physical contact and the setting a couple places themselves in are important factors in avoiding temptations. So the guidelines have to be drawn early enough so as not to get so excited and so involved sexually that they reach a point that it's difficult, if not impossible, to stop.[1]

8. *Write your mutual decision down on paper.* Again, be specific. This is necessary to eliminate misunderstanding or power

struggles. If both persons have verbally agreed that his hand under her blouse is "too far," and that limit has been written down, then neither individual can claim they didn't understand the boundary. Agreeing in writing, too, makes it easier to recognize manipulation, impulsiveness, and selfish motivation. Writing limits together is like shining a spotlight on that area of a relationship. It will immediately become clear to both individuals when the limit becomes a problem. If it never becomes a problem, there may never be a need to discuss it again. As long as the mutual limits are respected, the couple can relax and respond freely and spontaneously, knowing that their sexual relationship is preparing them for a healthy marriage.

9. *As you apply these steps to your relationship, remember to affirm your love for one another.* It will be important to remind one another regularly of your love, especially at times when one of you is feeling insecure or distant—a time when temptation may be intensified for that person. The motivation for making these decisions is your love for your partner and your commitment to the relationship. As you eliminate sexual behavior, you'll have the need and the opportunity to increase other forms of communicating your love. Thoughtful behaviors, small and meaningful gifts, and verbal expressions of love will deepen in significance.

10. *If you or your partner are continually crossing the boundaries or continually pushing the limits, do not ignore or minimize the implication of that behavior.* This should be a blaring signal that the relationship is not developing in the way that both of you have agreed upon. If you find yourselves consciously ignoring your mutually agreed-upon standards, repeatedly putting yourselves into situations that create trouble with temptations, then it's time to evaluate your motivation. You may need to face the fact that you are not particularly interested in the development of your relationship, but mainly in physical pleasure or gratification. Your behavior is an indication that commitment, motivation, or communication is not

what it should be and will cause significant problems later on. In this case, all the insight, information, and strategies in the world won't help your relationship grow beyond this point. As the old saying goes, *"You gotta wanna."*

Ask yourselves, are we really concerned about the relationship, or is our concern mainly for self-gratification? Self-gratification is an obviously inadequate basis for marriage. You may have to admit that this relationship is a poor prospect for marriage, either because of the impulsiveness of each of you, or the disregard one of you has for the other's values. Whatever the reason, it is much better to discover these problems prior to the marriage and postpone or cancel the wedding plans than to set yourselves up for serious marital problems that will be extremely difficult and painful to resolve later.

Wherever you choose to set your limits, any behavior will become boring and mundane if your sole purpose in physical contact is to experience sexual excitement. Remember that sexual arousal is progressive. It draws you into more and more involvement. A kiss, for example, soon becomes dull if your focus is the excitement you experience when you touch lips. You can prevent kissing from becoming routine if your conscious purpose is to express your feelings to your partner. A kiss will always remain meaningful if it is a form of communication rather than a method of self-gratification. Also, if your kiss is an honest expression of love, that love will never force itself past your agreed-upon boundaries in order to feel good. First Corinthians 13:5 reminds us that true love is not self-seeking. Remember that whatever limits you decide upon as a couple, there is no one to apply them but the two of you—no parents, no teachers, no pastors, no friends—no one but you. Remember, also, that being accountable to one another is an extremely important skill to bring to a marriage.

I ask each couple I work with, "Tell me what it was like to discuss setting physical boundaries and how has it affected your relationship?" Some say it was easy; many say it was awkward and difficult. The vast majority have said that once they discussed their honest feelings and convictions and made their decisions regarding limits, their relation-ship became much more relaxed. Many describe it as a turning point in their feelings of closeness. They no longer worried about what the other was thinking. They suddenly felt much more secure, and they all reported a sense of deepened intimacy without the complications of deepening their physical involvement. Never has anyone even hinted that he or she regretted having the discussion.

Two Facts to Remember

Two important principles underlie all that's been written here about taking steps to maintain sexual purity. First, for most individuals, the desire for sex is actually a desire for closeness and intimacy. The most sexually active single people are usually the loneliest. As was discussed in chapter 2, sex feels intimate, but since it can actually be a substitute for intimacy, it does not satisfy for long. By focusing on emotional intimacy and honest communication, the tendency toward sexual com-pulsion decreases.

Second, sex is progressive; it builds upon itself. The single person or the couple who gives in to sexual temptation will find it more difficult to resist the next time. By not giving in to temptation, it becomes less and less powerful. By avoiding sexual behavior as well as sexually arous-ing material, sexual tension will be reduced, not increased, over time.

I Can't Imagine Feeling Clean Again

Nancy was a twenty-two-year-old woman with a serious concern. We never met; my contact with her was limited to a telephone call she made to a live radio broadcast I was doing. But Nancy represents many people. Here's what she said: "I don't know what to do now. I'd give anything to be able to just erase the last nine years of my life. After losing my virginity at thirteen, I figured, what's the difference? I've got nothing left to lose. I've gotten involved sexually whenever I felt like it and often when I didn't. Now I've had three abortions, and I've slept with so many men I can't count them all. I've wanted so badly to be loved, and I'm realizing that no man has ever really loved me. Through some Christian friends, I'm learning that there is a better way, but how do I go back? I feel so dirty and used that I can't imagine feeling clean again. What can I do?"

There is hope for Nancy. There's hope for other women and men who, like Nancy, are casualties of the sexual revolution. While a person's sexual virginity can't be restored, people and situations can change. A person can minimize and even eliminate many of the negative patterns described in this book. It's never too late.

We choose whether our past mistakes and failures strengthen and develop our character. We're never trapped by our past if we're willing to change. Each of us has the capability of growing and becoming stronger, regardless of our experiences—sometimes *because of them.*

The first thing Nancy needed to understand was forgiveness. Although Nancy's behavior had caused her a multitude of problems, the Bible tells us that her sin is no less forgivable than any other. In James 2:10–11 we are told, "For whoever keeps the whole law and yet stumbles at just one point is guilty of breaking all of it. For he who said, 'Do not commit adultery,' also said, 'Do not murder.' If you do not commit adultery but do commit murder, you have become a lawbreaker.'" This may sound hopeless until one realizes that the death of Christ on the cross paid for *all* sins. Because of Christ's sacrifice, God offers forgiveness to everyone, regardless of the crime.

How did Jesus deal with sexual sin in others? Read the story in John 8. The woman's crime was adultery; the Law required her death. After assuring her that He didn't condemn her, Christ's instruction was, "Go now and leave your life of sin" (John 8:11).

God does not become angry and reject you when you fail. He is always holding you close and expecting your success, regardless of your feelings of failure. The dangerous tendency for people like Nancy is to become preoccupied with their mistakes. But focusing on failure is no solution—it only intensifies feelings of guilt and drives a person back to her or his problem behavior.

If you're in a situation similar to Nancy's, focus on your failure only long enough to fully understand what needs to change. Make yourself aware of early warning signs so that you'll recognize when the problem begins to recur.

Here are four steps to follow in dealing with unwise sexual choices of the past:

1. *Agree that you have violated God's standards.* Nothing can change until you take responsibility for your part in the behavior. Call it sin; don't blame anyone else. God is not surprised. "We all, like sheep, have gone astray, each of us has turned to his own way; and the LORD has laid on him the iniquity of us all" (Isa. 53:6).

2. *Choose to believe God's promise of forgiveness.* The penalty for your sin was paid in full at Calvary. You need only to lay claim to it. "If we confess our sins, he is faithful and just to forgive us our sins and purify us from all unrighteousness" (1 John 1:9).

3. *Choose to forgive yourself.* Read through Romans 8 several times and think about what it says about you. Don't buy into guilt trips. If God has forgiven you, you are forgiven. Forgiving yourself means accepting your humanness and agreeing that Christ did the whole job of redemption on the cross. You cannot supplement His work with your own suffering or self-pity.

4. *Choose to make a change.* This chapter has discussed methods to help you change behavior that prevents the building of healthy physical relationships. Make some decisions about how you will handle your relationships differently. Determine to change old patterns.

It is possible to have the relationship you desire. No matter what your past has been, your future can be different. But remember that healthy, growing, fulfilling relationships don't happen by accident. They are the result of decisions, commitment, and hard work. The first decision must be made by you as an individual. I strongly encourage you to invest your time in the steps suggested in this chapter. Getting started may be uncomfortable, but consider the pay-off on your investment—healthy sexual patterns for yourself and your future spouse.

Karlyn's Thoughts
Then One Thing Led to Another

Imagine you live in a hole. A small, dark, damp, smelly hole so deep down in the ground that the sky is only a marble-sized dot of baby blue, way up there somewhere. You'd really like to climb out and see what a whole skyful of blue looks like. But climbing out would take a lot of work. You'd have to make your own steel picks and then jam them into the wall, one above the other, slowly inching up toward freedom. Even though you've got the stuff needed to make the spikes, you tell yourself there's really no reason to leave your hole. You've got a bed, and food, and the atmosphere really isn't *that* bad. And besides, these steel links you make to pass the time take a lot less effort to forge then those sharp picks.

So you continue your days in that hole, working away at the bellows turning out steel objects, most of them chain links. Once, when you got really ambitious, you worked on a climbing pick. Maybe someday you'll get out of here, you think. But you quickly went back to making your links. Those picks are too hard to fashion; the sharp points take too much time to pound out.

Then one day, someone crawls into the hole. You're too busy at the bellows to notice him, but this creepy-looking guy is prowling around your stuff. He rifles through the pile of steel links you've created. It looks like he's linking them together, making one big long chain. He's looping it slowly, quietly around your ankle. Your waist. Your neck. But you're just at your work, unaware. There you stand, pounding out link after link after link. All the while, he keeps adding to the chain each link created until you can hardly move to make another one. Only when he anchors the chain to the ground with the only pick you forged, do you notice him—just as he moves to devour you. Too bad you didn't spend more time on those climbing picks, friend.

So what's the point of this bizarre story? It is to ask a question: Are we prepared for the enemy when he comes to tempt us? When he comes, will he find us with a ready-made chain just waiting to be wrapped around our neck . . . or will he find us halfway up the dirt wall, equipped with enough picks to climb our way to the top?

Let me share with you five essentials that I've found in trying to stay out of the traps of impurity.

First, *absolutely lose yourself in Jesus.* Pursue a friendship with Him. Read the Bible; find out what His disciples had to say about Him; learn the workings of His heart by finding out how He responded to what life threw at Him. Talk to Him—a lot. The more you get to know Jesus, the more He makes a lot of sense; and the more you'll truly want what His heart desires for you. Besides, He's the best friend you'll ever have. He's got your back covered wherever you go! Satan knows that you belong to Jesus, and the more you stay within His reach, the less the enemy will be willing to mess with you. He knows that our God is a jealous God. Let's not distance ourselves from our God's protection. Wake up each morning and ask Him to protect you from impurity that day—and then every time it rears its ugly head, pray for its defeat. Neglect to build this friendship with Jesus and you've forged the first link in your chain.

The next thing to remember is this: *strength is not always shown in staying to fight.* When you find yourself being tempted, *run.* Don't attempt to persevere within the temptation. You are *not* strong enough to survive any sexually stimulating situation that you get yourself into. So many battles have been lost this way; every little battle is a piece of the war. We can't settle for claiming an *almost* victory. Losing by a little isn't much of a consolation; it's still a loss. This battle is already ours, but we *must* claim the victory: "How we thank God, who gives us victory over sin and death through Jesus Christ our Lord!" (1 Cor. 15:57 NLT). Know your boundaries and vow to keep them. Don't entertain even for a split second any thought of fudging.

One summer my boyfriend and I had been staying up really late. So, when school started again, we gave ourselves a curfew of one o'clock, but we weren't very good about keeping the curfew. Then we started having trouble sticking to our physical boundaries and were wondering why we were having so much trouble with them—until we realized that all our issues were coming up after one o'clock. Compromises really *do* matter, even if they're seemingly little ones. "Be careful! Watch out for attacks from the Devil, your great enemy. He prowls around like a roaring lion, looking for some victim to devour" (1 Peter 5:8 NLT). He's watching like a tense predator, just waiting for you to leave one weak spot open—and he'll attack you right there, right where you've let him get a claw hold. You have the power to smash his attempts at destroying you—you've just got to claim it. "So humble yourselves before God. Resist the Devil, and he will flee from you" (James 4:7 NLT). Put the extra elbow grease into pounding out that point in your climbing pick—it will get you out of this hole a lot faster than a heavy chain will.

The next essential has become the foundation for everything else I'll ever figure out about relationships: *Being in a relationship is not about you.* When my focus isn't about what I want to *get* but instead is about what I'm *giving* I've noticed I get frustrated with my boyfriend a lot less. I think this happens for two reasons: (1) I'm not totally dwelling on what I want, so if I don't get it it's not quite such a big deal; and (2) when my energy is being poured into loving him instead of picking out everything he's doing wrong, it makes it easier for him to spend *his* energy freely loving me. Just imagine what could happen if both you and your significant other were each pouring 110 percent into the other person. There wouldn't be much room left for deficits, would there? Try it! I think you'll be surprised at what happens to your relationship. And here's a practical suggestion for how to start this kind of selfless love: *refuse to tempt.*

Refuse to tempt him. *Refuse* to tempt her. You've been brought together to work as a team, so don't disable your teammate by drawing her or him across the line. *You are in this relationship to protect this person;* determine to do it well. This means that my job is *not* to let my boyfriend cross a line during a weak moment—even if I want to cheat on that boundary, too. If I give signals like it would be okay to keep going, I'm tempting him while he's weak, kicking him while he's down. I know that in the morning he'd sorely regret the compromise; so instead of giving in, I get to help him retain strength. We're a team, remember? We're not out for personal gain; we want to make sure this team works as well as it possibly can.

The fourth essential is: *when you fall, get up again and keep going.* Yes, making picks is harder than making chains. Getting that sharp point just right is frustrating and time-consuming. Once in a while we might give up and turn out a chain link instead—maybe by letting ourselves entertain a quick racy daydream after we swore to stop fantasizing, or by talking to one of our girlfriends for an hour about marrying "him" even though we promised not to focus on that anymore. Good thing for us, one poor choice doesn't mean total failure. *Learn from your mistakes.* Yes, making a poor decision will make it harder to get back on track. Once I've tasted "the forbidden" it only gets harder to go back within my boundary again. But it's *not* impossible to get it right. Feel the cold steel chain against your neck and go back to making your climbing picks. Determine to *not* give in next time, and enlist your partner's help in doing it. If, for instance, things heat up too much between you two after you've watched a movie with suggestive scenes in it, don't watch that movie again. Decide together to protect each other. Discover your weaknesses, and then get rid of what triggers them.

The fifth essential to keeping purity in my relationship is to *always communicate.* How is my boyfriend supposed to be able to protect me if he doesn't know what I'm struggling with—and vice versa? Plus, if you've crossed a line, it's infinitely easier to decide what to do about that particular temptation when it's out in the open and you can work together to avoid it in the future. There was one time, shortly after we started kissing, that my boyfriend and I found ourselves French kissing—which was *way* beyond where we meant to go. As we talked about it later we counted five boundaries that we'd ignored. And though our make-out session lasted only an hour, it threw us for a loop for quite a bit longer. It took me more than two weeks before I could just kiss him without wanting to keep going! The thing is, if we hadn't talked about it, it probably would have happened again. I wasn't being incredibly successful in staying away from it; I really needed him to be strong. He wouldn't have known that if I didn't tell him. He might have thought I was okay with the whole thing, and then we would've been in *real* trouble. But instead, in the end, we came out victorious in that struggle—triumphant *as a team.*

These five essentials have been crucial in getting my relationship off to a strong start—and in keeping it healthy. I'm sure I'll find more things that are just as essential as I go along, but this is what I've got to offer right now. Wherever you are in your relationship, try to keep this in mind: What are you building right now? Chain links or climbing picks? Remember, *one thing leads to another.* What are your decisions leading to?

9

A very, very old message

"I've been a Christian for thirteen years, and I never knew the Bible said all that about sex." Marv was discussing his Bible class on sexuality and sexual expression. "I began this class expecting what I've always heard since I was a kid, all the 'Thou shalt nots'. . . . I'm really amazed." With a wink he added, "I'm discovering that God has a much better understanding of sex than I gave Him credit for."

Our world is full of beautiful things that God has created and we have misused. Look at the shores of polluted Lake Erie or the atmosphere of Los Angeles. Think of a piece of wood that can be used to either build a beautiful home or beat a man to death. Our imagination can be exquisitely creative or profoundly destructive. So it is with the gift of our sexuality. It's a two-sided coin—the beauty, excitement, and security of that expression of intimacy and trust is often perverted into a selfish, manipulative demand.

One of the dangers of the excitement side of the coin is to project preconceived ideas onto God. Bits and pieces of Scripture are read to find only the message that is assumed to be there. Many people are like Marv. They already "know" what the Bible says. Their parents told them. The pastor told them. It fits with what they "know" the rest of the Bible says. But they've never taken the time to really get into the Book. As a result, they end up getting everyone's opinion except God's.

This chapter examines the biblical view of sex. This is not meant to be an exhaustive Bible study; my goal is to crack open the door and encourage you to step into your own study of the topic. If you've never before studied Scripture regarding sexuality, you may be surprised at what you find.

A previous chapter discussed what the book of Genesis tells us about God's view of sex. Let's look a little further and see what we find.

The Song of Songs is an excellent illustration of God's attitude toward sexual expression. If you can get past the Hebrew symbolism, the message of the book is loud and clear. Here the young bride is describing her husband:

> Like an apple tree among the trees of the forest
>   is my lover among the young men.
> I delight to sit in his shade,
>   and his fruit is sweet to my taste.
> He has taken me to the banquet hall,
>   and his banner over me is love.
> Strengthen me with raisins,
>   refresh me with apples,
>   for I am faint with love.
> His left arm is under my head,
>   and his right arm embraces me.
> (Song of Songs 2:3–6)

Then the groom reflects upon his bride:

> Your neck is like the tower of David,
>   built with elegance;
> on it hang a thousand shields,
>   all of them shields of warriors.
> Your two breasts are like two fawns,
>   like twin fawns of a gazelle
>   that browse among the lilies.
> Until the day breaks

and the shadows flee,
I will go to the mountain of myrrh
    and to the hill of incense.
All beautiful you are, my darling;
    there is no flaw in you.

(Song of Songs 4:4–7)

When speaking to his bride, the groom says,

You are a garden locked up, my sister, my bride;
    you are a spring enclosed, a sealed fountain.
Your plants are an orchard of pomegranates
    with choice fruits . . .
and all the finest spices.

(Song of Songs 4:12–14)

To which his bride replies,

Awake, north wind,
    and come, south wind!
Blow on my garden,
    that it's fragrance may spread abroad.
Let my lover come into his garden
    and taste its choice fruits.

(Song of Songs 4:16)

Throughout the book the picture is of open, relaxed, fulfilling lovemaking between a young bride and groom who are free from guilt. Later in this chapter we'll come back to some of these passages and look at why there can be freedom from guilt.

scriptural warnings

Hebrews 13:4 is an interesting verse:

Marriage should be honored by all, and the marriage bed kept pure, for God will judge the adulterer and all the sexually immoral.

The Greek term translated as "bed" in this verse is the word *koite*. It is derived from the Latin word *cotio,* which gives our English word *coitus,* meaning sexual intercourse. This same word, in Romans 13:13 is translated "sexual indulgence and promiscuity." The message here is that sexual indulgence is promoted within marriage. Any negative reference to this term revolves around premarital sex (fornication) or extramarital sex (adultery). This is how the "marriage bed" is defiled; there is no other way.

First Timothy 4:4 tells us that everything that God created is good. Everything, however, is capable of being used for either good or evil purposes. The proper use of the good gift of sex is very clear: sex is promoted and encouraged within the stability of a marriage commitment, never outside of it. Within the loving marriage commitment, God gives no sexual restrictions at all.

The first nine chapters of Proverbs have a great deal to say about sexual expression. Proverbs 5:15–21 captures the message as well. This is a message of instruction from father to son, from history's wisest king to his adolescent prince. The topic is the proper use of the sex drive. Solomon uses picturesque language:

> Drink water from your own cistern,
>> running water from your own well.
> Should your springs overflow in the streets,
>> your streams of water in the public squares?
> Let them be yours alone,
>> never to be shared with strangers.
> May your fountain be blessed,
>> and may you rejoice in the wife of your youth.
> A loving doe, a graceful deer—
>> may her breasts satisfy you always,
>> may you ever be captivated by her love.

> Why be captivated, my son, by an adulteress?
>   Why embrace the bosom of another man's wife?
> For a man's ways are in full view of the LORD,
>   and he examines all his paths.
>
>   (Proverbs 5:15–21)

In verses 15–17 he's not talking about giving water to his neighbor's sheep. He's talking about enjoying sex with his wife. Verses 18–19 make this very clear. Sex is to be fully and luxuriously enjoyed . . . within the bounds of a lifetime commitment with one partner.

If we go back to verse 1, we can see the concern of the king for his son and the reason behind the writing of these instructions. He writes with the insight of "one who's been there":

> My son, pay attention to my wisdom,
>   listen well to my words of insight,
> that you may maintain discretion
>   and your lips may preserve knowledge.
> For the lips of an adulteress drip honey,
>   and her speech is smoother than oil;
> but in the end she is bitter as gall,
>   sharp as a double-edged sword.
> Her feet go down to death;
>   her steps lead straight to the grave.
> She gives no thought to the way of life;
>   her paths are crooked, but she knows it not.
>
> Now then, my sons, listen to me;
>   do not turn aside from what I say.
> Keep to a path far from her,
>   do not go near the door of her house,
> lest you give your best strength to others
>   and your years to one who is cruel,
> lest strangers feast on your wealth
>   and your toil enrich another man's house.

> At the end of your life you will groan,
> when your flesh and your body are spent.
> (Proverbs 5:1–11)

In the books of Leviticus and Deuteronomy, we read about the Law given to the Israelites by God. God was preparing the nation of Israel for a special task. He was going to use them to bring the Messiah to the world. His goal was to make them a successful and powerful nation. God knew that lax sexual standards would be disastrous to their society's development. He had a very effective method of discouraging promiscuity among young people. The rules went like this:

1. All adultery was punishable by the death of both the man and the woman (Lev. 20:10).
2. If a woman had intercourse prior to marriage and this fact was exposed on her wedding night, evidenced by the lack of a bloody sheet, she was to be executed (Deut. 22:13–21).
3. If a man had sex with an engaged woman, he would be stoned to death (Deut. 22:25–26).
4. If a man had intercourse with an unengaged virgin, he was forced to marry her and pay a dowry to her father (Deut. 22:28–29).

Think about those four laws for a moment. The penalties were severe, but they were a great method for promoting sexual accountability. We could assume that any woman who had lost her virginity prior to marriage would certainly not let the man involved get away with it. If she did, marriage to anyone else would mean the death sentence for her. If she never married, there was no place for her in Hebrew society, other than perhaps the life of a harlot. All in all, it sounds like an effective method of ensuring sexually pure courtship. These laws serve to illustrate for us the high value God places on sexual abstinence outside of marriage.

Let's turn again to the Song of Songs. As we pointed out earlier, this is an explicit book concerning the joys of married love. The book revolves around a relationship between Solomon and his bride,

Shulamith, both before and after their wedding. Included are their sexual experiences as well as dreams, fears, and fantasies. (For a thorough discussion and commentary on this book, I recommend reading *Solomon on Sex* by Joseph Dillow.)[1]

The bride repeats one phrase three times: "Do not arouse or awaken love until it so desires" (2:7; 3:5; 8:4). This phrase is primarily a warning against premarital sexual promiscuity. Its warning goes beyond that, however, and includes the arousal and excitement of sexual feelings for anyone but a committed life partner. That's an interesting statement for a discourse on sexual freedom.

The quote is found in the midst of love scenes. In these love scenes the bride is describing the beautiful, liberating experience of their love on the wedding night, and she relates that beauty and freedom to their premarital chastity. The message is that sexual involvement before the wedding may endanger the beauty of sex in marriage. This message puts the book into a moral context that is consistent with all of Scripture.

Considering the negative reputation the Bible has had regarding sexual issues, it's significant to note that every restriction in Scripture can be summed up in one precept: *sex should be kept within marriage.* If you have one sexual partner and you are committed to him or her for life within marriage, relax and enjoy one another in love.

While limitations are few, the warnings are powerful. God obviously places an extremely high premium on sexual purity. As discussed earlier, the Old Testament prescribed death as a resolution for sexual promiscuity. The New Testament also has some significant statements about the dangers of sexual indiscretions. The sexual standard in the New Testament is crystal clear: no premarital sex. It makes no distinction between casual sex, recreational sex, or sex between people who are "married in God's eyes." God leaves no room for such rationalizing or justifying. Let's take a closer look at the New Testament message.

In the Greek text, the word for both fornication and immorality is *porneia*. *Porneia* refers to sexual activity outside the bonds of marriage. It includes premarital sex, extramarital sex, homosexuality, and the whole gamut of sexual perversions. It is such a serious distortion of God's desire and plan that Christians are admonished not only to avoid any form of fornication (1 Thess. 4:3) but not even to talk about it (Eph. 5:3).

I won't take the space here to quote each of the passages listed, but I urge you to look them up and read them in their context. That way my comments will make much more sense:

- *1 Corinthians 5:9–13:* Paul warned the Corinthian church not to tolerate individuals who continually practiced *porneia,* but to ostracize them in judgment.

- *1 Corinthians 6:13–20:* The focus here is on the seriousness of illicit sexual intercourse because of its effects, both physically and spiritually. Paul uses the example of a harlot, but his focus is on the act, not who it's committed with. He could just as easily have referred to a coworker or a campus cheerleader.

- *1 Corinthians 10:8–13:* Paul explains that God dealt severely with sexual immorality in the Old Testament as an example for us who live in the last days. Verse 13 is a promise that God will not allow us to be overwhelmed by temptation. When God asks us to do something, He also guarantees that we are capable of doing it.

- *Galatians 5:16–21:* In the life of a Christian, illicit sexual intercourse is listed first among the deeds that are diametrically opposed to the Spirit of God. This passage is followed by the fruits of the Spirit, the first of which is love. The implication here may be that premarital sex as well as adultery is the opposite of love. Verse 21 states clearly that the practice of these acts keeps people from the kingdom of God. This is a warning that Paul repeats in 1 Corinthians 6:9–10 and Ephesians 5:5–6.

- *Colossians 3:5–6:* Paul assures us that the wrath of God will come as a result of *porneia.*

- *1 Thessalonians 4:1–8:* Paul warns that illicit sexual intercourse is the opposite of the will of God and that God is the avenger of sexual immorality.

conclusion

The story line of an Alfred Hitchcock TV episode illustrates an important point about life. The story begins with a woman who was found guilty of murder and sentenced to life imprisonment without parole. She vowed to escape her incarceration in any way possible and was constantly in search of a foolproof plan to gain her freedom.

During her imprisonment she became friends with the prison mortician, an elderly man with a chronic and severe health problem. It was this man's job to dispose of the remains of all inmates who died in prison. He built the casket, dug the grave, saw that the casket was buried; he did it all.

The woman assured the mortician that she could find and finance a complete cure for his painful ailment if only she could be free of the prison walls. She eventually convinced the mortician to help her escape in exchange for his cure.

The plan was that when the next funeral bell tolled, announcing the death of a prisoner, the woman would find her way to the morgue and climb into the casket with the corpse. The mortician would go about his normal duties of taking the casket outside the prison and burying it in the cemetery. Within a short period of time he would return and unearth the casket and free the woman. It was an impressive plan with great potential for success.

The plan went exactly as anticipated. The bell tolled, the woman went to the morgue, and she entered the dark casket with the newly deceased remains. She felt the casket being moved to the graveside, lowered into the ground, and covered with dirt. She waited and waited and waited; no mortician. It seemed like an eternity before, in desperation, she ventured to strike a match to determine the time elapsed in her waiting. In the light of the small flame she made a startling discovery. The body in the casket with her was that of her mortician friend.

Can you imagine the desperation and regret of this woman? The perfect plan, one single hitch. The result? Complete disaster.

So it is when we choose to ignore God's clear warnings to us in His Word. He has not given us a set of constraints—a set of rules and expectations that imprison us. Rather, He has lovingly provided a design for sexual fulfillment that frees us to know another intimately and in turn to be known intimately by that person. When we go our own way, all the plans, rationalizations, and excuses in the world will not change the results of violating His natural order.

The experiences shared in this book, as well as the patterns and problems discussed, are predictable, expected consequences of violating the purpose of the sexual relationship. God has blessed the human race with the capability to relate sexually. His purpose is pleasure, fulfillment, and closeness, as well as procreation. We can experience great joy and fulfillment by following God's design for sexual expression, or we can misuse His gift and suffer the consequences. The choice is ours.

Growing closer

1. Look up and read 1 Thessalonians 4:1–8. Using this passage as a foundation, can you think of any good reason for having premarital sex?
2. In your own words, how is God's love expressed through the scriptural restrictions on sexual expression?

Karlyn's Thoughts
Receiving the Real Treasure

> *You are like a private garden, my treasure,*
> *my bride! You are like a spring that no one else can drink*
> *from, a fountain of my own.*
> *(Song of Songs 4:12 nlt)*

There once was a little girl whose father doted on her ridiculously. He was forever giving her new toys, calling her his little princess, and taking her on outings—just the two of them. One thing he'd given her that she especially adored was a string of toy pearls. She wore them almost every day, and would prance about as if she really were a princess. Feeling the plastic beads slide between her fingers when she twirled the string around her neck made her feel as if she were the richest girl in the world.

Then one day, as her father was tucking her into bed, he asked her a strange question. "Honey, will you give me your pearls?"

"Oh no, Daddy, not my pearls," she quickly replied. "But you can have my favorite purple pony instead."

He seemed sad as he shook his head, smiled at her, and gently kissed her forehead before leaving the room. "Good night, Princess." The next night he asked the same strange question. "Honey, will you give me your pearls?"

The little girl was confused and upset that he'd asked again. "No, Daddy, I love my pearls. But you can have my favorite baby doll—the one with the soft blonde hair, if you want."

Again, her father's eyes were sad as he shook his head, smiled at her, and gently kissed her forehead before he left the room. "Good night, Princess."

The next night, the little girl wasn't waiting in bed for her father to come in. She was sitting up, her blue eyes full of tears, her little fingers clasped tightly around something she held in her lap. As her father walked into the room, she looked up and a big tear rolled down her flushed cheek. She held out her hand to him. "Here, Daddy," she whispered, uncurling her fingers, "you can have my pearls if you want them."

Her father's eyes misted as he lifted the beloved plastic necklace out of her hands and put it in his pocket. "Thank you, sweetheart," he told her, stroking her head as more tears made their way down her round little cheeks. Then, slowly, he reached inside his jacket pocket and pulled out a little velvet box. "Now," he said, his eyes dancing with delight as he watched her eyes fasten on the box, "I can give you this." And when she opened the box, there was the most gorgeous pearl necklace that money could buy. Her father had just been waiting for her to give up her toy so that he could give her the real thing.

I remember my first romantic relationship. I was a senior in high school when my "special friend" and I began to notice each other. We started hanging out a lot. I was always over at his house. We went to parties together. And before long, we became "unofficially official." Everyone knew that we liked each other. We had a DTR (a define-the-relationship talk) and decided to remain just friends, but I desperately wanted more than that. I was sure that *this* was the guy I was supposed to marry, and eventually he'd get the picture and fall madly in love with me and everything would be dandy. So I clung to that hope and spent the better part of eleven long months and untold amounts of energy trying to reel him in.

Except that God kept asking me to give him up. I didn't want to hear Him, but at the same time I knew *exactly* what He was saying. And I never had the guts to straight-out tell God *no;* so I would tell Him, "Sure, I'll give him up . . . as long as you'll give him back." Have you ever done that? It didn't work out so well. God knew what He was talking about. The whole relationship just kept getting more and more frustrating, and I kept getting more and more irritated. Then finally, after eleven months, it ended—having never actually been official. I finally let go in June (actually, that he was "torn out of my grip" might be a more accurate description).

I gave up my feelings for him in trust that God had something else in mind for me. But what was it? *Nothing* was happening. Then six months later, in December, this other guy started to notice me. Through an unusual series of events, God very obviously brought us together. We're not perfect, and I don't know if we'll be together for the rest of our lives, although that's a definite possibility. We've worked hard to show each other real love, respect, and understanding—all mixed in with our unusual personalities and molded to fit our even more unusual pairing. And to think that I almost missed out on this treasure by refusing to give up the plastic necklace that *I* wanted to hang on to! I'm so thankful for the reward God blessed me with. I can tell you from my own experience, His rewards are real—most of the time you have to wait for them, but they're more real than anything you're trying to create by yourself. Be willing to look forward to something better. Let yourself trust—and be surprised.

What kinds of relationship imitations can you see in your life? I have one example. Let's say that you're a girl, and that you and your significant other have been dating for a long time. Things have been going great: you find security in him, you make him feel needed, and you certainly couldn't imagine life without each other. But lately, all you ever seem to do when you're together is either make out and experiment or get into petty arguments—even big, screaming fights. When you're getting physical everything seems fine and lovey-dovey again. But those in-between times make you think that something doesn't quite match up. If that sounds familiar, you could be settling for less than you deserve. Premarital sexual involvement is rarely sex at its best. It's an imitation. A fake. Would you give it up? Would you give up the pleasure now for the assurance that God wants you to be happier than you ever dreamed possible? Would you believe Him if He offered you a *true* love?

> Jesus replied, "People soon become thirsty again after drinking this water. But the water I give them takes away thirst altogether. It becomes a perpetual spring within them, giving them eternal life." (John 4:13–14 NLT)

Jesus was talking to a woman whose life had been steeped in sexual sin—with five divorces under her belt and now with a live-in boyfriend, she'd tried hard to find a love that was real. Then finally Someone came along who could actually offer it to her. The relationship that God wants to bring into your life is full of life, laughter, honesty, trust, tenderness, truth. It's *real*. First He'll teach you to love Him; then He'll teach you to love another human being. With only the promise of a future reward, could you trust enough now to let go of your plastic necklace?

> The water I give them takes away thirst altogether. (v. 14 NLT)

Guys, what do you ultimately want out of a relationship? A wife, right? And not just *any* wife. A woman who knows how to love you with every fiber of her being. Someone who, day after day, puts herself aside to serve you just because she loves to make you happy. Now, would you rather try and pick her out yourself—or let God do it for you? Let me put that question in another setting. Let's say you've just been offered a choice—one of several huge piles of jewels stocked away in a storeroom. The only catch is that most of the piles are made up of fakes; only a couple of piles contain real jewels. And most of the *imitation* gems are extremely well-concealed as the real thing. Now you have a decision to make. Do you try and weed out the fakes yourself? Or do you ask the world-renowned jewel expert standing beside you to tell you which ones to pick out?

> Who can find a virtuous and capable wife? She is worth more than precious rubies. Her husband can trust her, and she will greatly enrich his life. She will not hinder him but help him all her life. (Proverbs 31:10–12 NLT)

Alright, now girls: What are we looking for in a relationship? Eventually a husband, right? But even more than that, we're looking for a husband who's going to be in love with us with all of his heart for the rest of our lives. I don't know about you, but *I* want a man who is totally and completely captivated by me, someone who's so head-over-heels in love that sometimes he can't see which way is up. Someone who routinely puts himself aside just because he loves to see me happy. Doesn't that sound exhilarating? To be *adored*.

> You have ravished my heart, my treasure, my bride. I am overcome by one glance of your eyes, by a single bead of your necklace. How sweet is your love, my treasure, my bride! How much better it is than wine! Your perfume is more fragrant than the richest of spices. (Song of Songs 4:9–10 NLT)

This guy is so in love that just one glance at her *jewelry* sends him into ecstasy. Do you think *you* can find a man like that? Would you bet the rest of your life on that decision? *Or* would you rather turn the choice over to the One who has power over the future? The One who can see *both* of you in twenty, thirty, fifty years, the One who knows who's going to adore you as much when you're forty-five as he adores you now at eighteen or twenty-five?

We have a very dim view of what makes us happy, of what makes us fulfilled. While we cling to plastic imitations of our dreams, our Father is nearly bursting with excitement at the treasures He has in store for us as soon as we turn our toys over to Him. He wants to take the fake love away. He wants to prepare us and teach us how to love for *real*—and He wants to give us someone whom He's also taught about real love. In that partnership you'll learn what it means to have a *real* relationship, and you'll wonder why you even hesitated to give up your imitation.

Hindsight is 20/20. Let trust in our God and let His promises be your foresight.

afterword

While completing the final manuscript for this book, I met a young married couple with an encouraging story to tell. Although there are many more details than I can share here, I include only a portion of their experience because it illustrates so well the purpose of this book. I'm grateful to them for allowing us to "peek in" on their experience as a couple.

Doug and Kathy met while in college. They fell in love almost immediately and were soon spending every spare minute together. Since they both assumed that before long they'd be sleeping together, they discussed and planned for their contraceptives, and went together to purchase them. They made that night as romantic as possible. Their communication was good and their goal was to do everything correctly. That night was the enjoyable beginning of an active sex life that was satisfying to both of them.

After a number of months, however, dissatisfaction began to creep in. Something just wasn't right. For some time, Doug and Kathy could escape the tension with sex. But even this area of their relationship became dissatisfying to them. They tried sexual abstinence, thinking "It will get better if we stop for a while." They began to experience a lack of real intimacy, although neither was sure what the problem was or what to do about it.

In the midst of this confusion, Kathy was confronted with the idea that sex before marriage was sin. Although they had no concept of Christ's forgiveness or of personal salvation, Doug and Kathy considered themselves Christians, and since they did not consider themselves hypocrites, the idea of premarital sex as sin helped confirm their decision of abstinence.

Both Doug and Kathy had attended church in childhood. In more recent years they had become acquainted with a variety of religious experiences, from passive involvement in various churches to experimenting with the New Age Movement. When they were invited to attend church by a Christian friend, both felt comfortable attending. The message of the morning was from the book of Jonah, and the topic was "running from God." It was a sermon that hit both of them right between the eyes. That evening, after a long and tearful discussion with their Christian friend, both Doug and Kathy accepted Christ as their Savior and Lord.

While their new spiritual awareness was exciting to both of them, they still struggled with sexual desires. Now, more than ever, they were keenly aware that God wanted them to continue in sexual abstinence. They made a commitment to one another and even wrote it down together. They called it "Seven Ground Rules for Love":

1. If it doesn't please and glorify God, it has no place in our relationship; He is the head of our love.
2. When we feel the pressure building, we will put some space between us.
3. When we get too wrapped up in each other, we will turn our eyes and open our hearts to Christ.
4. Certain fondling and intimacy is reserved for the sanctity of marriage.
5. A hug will serve the purpose of communicating our love for each other.
6. We will strive to communicate the love we share, rather than our physical attraction to each other.
7. When we struggle with this, we will remember that Jesus can and will help us if we only stop and ask Him.

After writing this commitment together, both Kathy and Doug signed it and kept it where it could be referred to whenever necessary.

Maintaining their commitment was extremely difficult. They shared many emotional conversations while working through insecurities, fears, and forgiveness. There were times when the emotional struggle seemed beyond their ability to handle. Through all their difficulties, their commitment to the relationship remained strong, as did their commitment to sexual purity. More than two years after their decision for sexual abstinence, Doug and Kathy married.

Not long before their wedding, they were shopping for lingerie for the wedding night. As Kathy looked at the sexy negligees, she realized she'd never really enjoyed wearing them. In the past, she'd bought and worn them to please Doug, but she was more comfortable in long, cozy, warm nightgowns. Her deep desire for Doug's satisfaction, however, kept her looking through the rack of lingerie.

"Which do you like, Doug?" she asked over her shoulder.

"Y'know, I really don't like any of those," he replied. "Don't you think you'd be more comfortable in this one? It's more your style, and I think you'd look great in it."

Kathy turned to see Doug holding a long white flannel nightgown. As tears clouded her eyes, several things became very clear to Kathy. The nightgown signified Doug's love and his understanding of her needs, while its color signified her desire for restored sexual purity. Through their commitment and frustrations of the past two years, they'd become very much in tune with each other. They had learned to communicate in ways they'd never known possible.

Their wedding night was full of discoveries. After more than two years of sexual abstinence, both found themselves extremely nervous but reassured as they realized this was what a wedding night should be like. In Kathy's words, "I was nervous, and I *loved* it."

Kathy made another discovery on the wedding night. Her previous experiences of intercourse had never resulted in orgasm. She assumed that her sexual experience was as physically fulfilling as it could possibly be. She was quite shocked and pleased to discover there was more.

Another confirming experience for them on the wedding night was that Kathy experienced the pain and light bleeding typical of a first sexual experience. Although others may disagree, Kathy is convinced this was God's assurance of her restored innocence and purity.

Doug and Kathy have no regrets regarding their premarital commitment to abstinence. In spite of their early missteps, this couple found hope. The foundation of that hope was their desire to follow the Lord in response to their newfound salvation. Their obedience brought healing and growth to their relationship.

It is my prayer that this book can help others discover what this couple found.

Appendix:
"Hello, Doctor . . . ?"

Sarah came to my office anxious and preoccupied. As a working divorced parent, she had a great deal to think about even without her current crisis: her sixteen-year-old daughter, Julie, had just given birth to a five-pound girl. Life was about to change drastically for all of them.

This situation was not new to Sarah. Her own mother had been pregnant before she was married. That marriage had lasted for a miserable thirty-five years. The entire family still suffered from it, even though the children were grown and Sarah's father had died several years ago. Her oldest brother, Glenn, still bitterly expressed his resentment over being the cause and victim of that disastrous marriage.

Sarah married Tom after finding out that she was pregnant. At eighteen years of age she was anxious to get away from her parents, and she fell madly in love with Tom. Looking back, she realizes that neither of them was ready for marriage. Tom left two years after their daughter was born, and Sarah hasn't heard from him since.

Now the pattern has repeated itself in a third generation. "I can't get Julie to understand how serious this is," Sarah was saying. "Her boyfriend is denying that it's his child and will have nothing to do with Julie now. She keeps saying that everything will be fine, but she doesn't see how much better it *could* have been." Sarah's emotions seemed to turn off as she continued, "I was planning to take some computer classes next semester. I was hoping to get promoted and finally have a little extra cash. Now all that will have to wait for at least a few years. I was hoping that Julie could go to college and have a better life than we've had, but that isn't likely now. I don't think we can afford much day care. I'll probably need to cut back at work to care for the baby so Julie can at least finish high school."

The trauma of unwanted pregnancy is often underestimated by most young people. Unwed mothers in the United States number well over one million annually. Each year more than thirty thousand girls under age fifteen become mothers. Some studies estimate that 40 percent of today's fourteen-year-old girls will become pregnant before they are twenty years old.[1] These are staggering statistics. The negative effects of these patterns are monumental to our nation, to our families, to the next generation, and most important, to the unwed mothers and their children.

The majority of young mothers in the United States live below the poverty level. Only one half of these girls who give birth before age eighteen complete high school (96 percent of girls without children complete high school in the United States).[2] Seventy-one percent of women under age thirty who receive welfare had their first child before age twenty. Children living with single mothers are six to seven times more likely to live in poverty than children in an intact family.[3] This pattern of unwed childbirth is often called the hub of the U.S. poverty cycle. The Center for Population Options estimates that in the past ten years the cost of support to unwed mothers in America has doubled from $8 billion to $17 billion, and it continues to rise.

Beyond the financial costs, the babies of unwed mothers have extremely high rates of illness and death. As they grow, they're far more likely than other children to experience educational, emotional, and behavioral problems. The rate of child abuse among these children is far above the national average.

It would seem that the most immediate answer to the problem of unwed pregnancy is the use of contraceptives. During the past thirty years, contraceptives have been developed, improved, promoted, and distributed. Today, over-the-counter contraceptives such as emergency oral contraceptive pills, condoms, foams, and sponges are available to anyone of any age. After over three decades of freely available contraceptives, however, the instances of unwed pregnancy have not decreased. In fact, most statistics indicate that the problem is significantly worse than thirty years ago.

The major problem with contraceptive use among young single people is that it is done irresponsibly or not at all. The prevalent attitude in our culture seems to be counterproductive, there being a double standard among singles regarding sexual activity. On the one hand, virginity is considered immature and unsophisticated. At the same time, *preplanned* illicit sex is somehow immoral. To be swept away by passion is understandable, forgivable, and even desirable, but to plan ahead for sex by using a contraceptive is considered bad or at least boring. One person expressed the attitude well when she said, "If I did use a contraceptive, then I'd have sex more. Then it would be too easy. . . . I don't feel it's right. I haven't been raised that way."

This attitude is strongly substantiated by the people I counsel. I'm surprised by the number of single people who are supposedly "sophisticated" and sexually "liberated" but who, when they're honest, experience a deep sense of guilt over the use of contraceptives. This seems to be especially true of women, who want to avoid the stigma of being loose or available; if a woman is taking a pill every day or carrying a diaphragm in her purse—"just in case"—she'll sooner or later have to face the fact that these unflattering terms apply to her.

Most people don't like, of course, to think of themselves as statistics. Most sexually active singles don't plan on getting pregnant, yet many of them seldom use contraceptives. Most single pregnant women expected, or at least hoped, that they would beat the odds. There are certainly exceptions to the statistics, but they are rare. The single woman who discovers that she's pregnant has four options. Whichever one she chooses will profoundly change her life forever and the lives of many other people. She may:

1. marry in order to provide a two-parent home for the child;
2. raise the child alone (perhaps marry in the future);
3. abort the child before birth;
4. place the child up for adoption.

Let's take a look at some of the consequences of these options.

premature marriages

In most instances, marriage because of pregnancy creates serious problems. A couple's developing relationship is short-circuited as they are forced into parental roles they have not anticipated or prepared for. They often start resenting each other and the child. Behind that resentment are almost always deep feelings of failure and frustration at having had to change life plans, goals, and ideals. The needs of the child compounded with the needs of each partner result in demands that are greater than most young relationships can bear.

These marriages do not always end in divorce, but communication is seldom well developed, or if it was good at one time, it usually deteriorates. Conflicts often are not resolved, and the potential for unfaithfulness in both partners is multiplied. Resentment, regret, and guilt become an inherent part of the marriage. Everyone loses. The biggest loss of all is experienced by the innocent child born without choice or preparation for the situation. While professional therapy can be extremely beneficial for these marriages, most young couples don't seek counseling.

unwed parenthood

While there are exceptions, usually the fathers involved in premarital pregnancies are absent, uninvolved, or disinterested. A generation ago it was assumed that a couple would marry if the woman was pregnant. Although the resulting marriage was usually less than satisfying, the emphasis was on responsibility, not satisfaction. Today, unmarried fathers seldom contribute financially to their children's support.

Many studies have shown that families headed by young mothers are far more likely to be living below the poverty line than other families. The resulting hardships are reflected in the statistics quoted earlier, but the difficulties go far beyond statistics. Besides the financial hardships, the individuals involved often have a very unrealistic concept of motherhood (or fatherhood). Even in an ideal marriage, time, patience, energy, and hard work are necessary to care for a child. Add financial strain; loss of a relationship; change in life plans; fears of dependency; feelings of abandonment, guilt, and failure, and you can begin to see the complexity of unwed parenthood.

Often forgotten in the statistics are the grandparents of the new baby, although they figure very significantly in the picture. Frequently the pregnant woman's parents end up in a role of support they hadn't planned on and may resent. Their own dreams must die if they desire to adequately support their daughter.

Sometimes competition develops between grandparent and mother as to "who knows best" and who raises the child. The feelings of the new mother toward her parents are mixed. It is not unusual for her to feel a blend of gratitude and resentment. This causes additional strain at a time when energy and patience levels are low for everyone involved.

The Abortion Deception

It is a sad fact that in our society abortion is another option for the unwed mother. As controversial as abortion is, it's the option chosen in an overwhelming number of cases. In 2000, 1.3 million American women obtained abortions. This amounts to about 21 percent of all pregnancies. This year more than one million teenage girls (under twenty years of age) will become pregnant. That's more than 3,000 every day. Almost half of these girls will have abortions. At current rates, about one in three American women will have had an abortion by the time she reaches age forty-five. This correlates with a number of studies showing that 50 percent of unwanted pregnancies in the United States end in abortion. This mass murder of unborn human beings is a sad commentary on our society's values.

A further tragedy in regard to these statistics is that the consequences of abortion are significantly misrepresented, minimized, or ignored by abortion's supporters and are seldom presented to the prospective mother. Abortion is viewed by many as no more than a simple medical procedure. This is so far from the truth. Emotional and spiritual trauma is the rule rather than the exception for the would-be mother.

A study by Dr. Anne Speckhard, cited in *Why Wait?*, shows many of the long-term (5–10 years later) emotional consequences of abortion. Of the women interviewed in that study

- 81 percent reported preoccupation with the aborted child;
- 73 percent reported flashbacks of the abortion experience;
- 69 percent reported feelings of "craziness" after the abortion;
- 54 percent recalled nightmares related to the abortion;
- 35 percent reported visitations from her aborted child;
- 23 percent reported hallucinations related to the abortion.[4]

In Dr. Speckhard's findings, 72 percent of the subjects said they held no religious beliefs at the time of their abortions and 96 percent in retrospect regarded abortion as the taking of life or as murder.

Abortion is far more than a medical procedure or political currency. Abortion has profound effects—emotional, psychological, and spiritual—that must not be ignored. While a thorough evaluation of the topic is beyond the scope of this book, many other fine books do deal with it. One I recommend is *Abortion's Second Victim* by Pam Corbel, published by Victor Books. The author does a thorough job of explaining some of the popular notions and myths surrounding abortion. She offers, too, personal insight for those who need help in healing the hurts associated with abortion.

The Adoption option

The long-range consequences of adoption tend to be fewer and less severe than those associated with the other options. It is often the most positive option because it generally provides a loving home for the child as well as medical care and emotional support for the mother. But adoption is by no means an easy decision to make. Mothers who have given their newborn child to adoptive parents generally express a deep feeling of loss. A period of grieving is experienced, as there would be in any significant loss.

Premarital pregnancy, with its far-reaching and tragic consequences, is only one side of the double-edged sword of premarital sex. The other edge is just as devastating and can be a deadly reminder of wrong choices.

Sexually Transmitted Diseases

Premarital sex always carries the threat of STDs. The impact of this consequence, like that of pregnancy, goes far beyond the sexually involved couple. Friends, family, and future sexual partners are deeply affected as are any children who might be born. Also affected is the medical community, which treats the massive number of cases each year, as well as the insurance industry and welfare system that pay for that diagnosis and treatment. In some cases the diagnosis is equally as expensive, if not more so, than the treatment. Our society thus suffers profoundly from the effects of this sexual consequence— the results of people making individual decisions regarding sexual standards.

Karen was an attractive, single, twenty-four-year-old flight attendant. Although she was very popular socially and had many boyfriends, she had been involved sexually only twice, both times with men she cared for deeply.

"I can't believe it." Karen's words could hardly be understood through her sobbing. "I just can't believe it. Why would God let this happen? What am I going to do?"

A few hours before our discussion, her family doctor had diagnosed her as having contracted genital herpes. She understood there was no cure for the disease, and that she had the potential to pass it on for the remainder of her life to any person with whom she engaged in sex. The desperation of her words still echo in my memory: "What healthy Christian man is going to risk marriage with me now? If only . . ."

Every day thousands of individuals contract STDs. For them there are no quiet words of reassurance to make the problem go away.

Many STDs are occurring in epidemic proportions and frequently coexist. According to an estimate by the American Social Health Association, someone in America contracts an STD every three seconds. Roughly 30,000 new cases of STDs are reported every day. After the common cold, gonorrhea and syphilis are, in fact, two of the most common infectious diseases in the United States. This is no small problem, considering the possible effects. Several of the STDs have no cure or even treatment. Many end in death.

As I talk with people in my practice, as well as in my teaching, I'm often amazed at their ignorance concerning these diseases. In a culture that promotes sexual activity as intensely as ours does, we have carefully avoided discussing the obvious dangers and health hazards that go hand-in-hand with a sexually liberal lifestyle. To some degree, the results of that ignorance are the diseases discussed in the remainder of this chapter.

By no means will this be an exhaustive discussion of all health hazards related to sexual behavior. It is meant to be only a brief description and reference for the major or most common STDs. If you have any of the symptoms described here, or if you have any reason to believe you've contracted an STD, consult your healthcare provider and explain your fears. Don't hesitate; not one of these diseases is worth ignoring.

If some of the terms and descriptions are unclear to you, I recommend reading *Intended for Pleasure* by Ed Wheat and Gaye Wheat for illustrations and descriptions of the functioning of male and female reproductive systems.[5]

General overview of sexually transmitted diseases

A few principles should be understood about STDs. First, if an individual is diagnosed with one STD, he or she most likely has at least one other STD, and often more. Infection with any STD increases the likelihood that an individual will acquire more STDs. This is because contracting one STD creates increased risk factors for contracting further STDs, plus the body's immune defense is lowered while it is working to control or eliminate an infection. A lowered immune system is especially true in the case of human immunodeficiency virus (HIV) infection, which causes acquired immune deficiency syndrome (AIDS). Second, STDs affect women at a much higher rate than men, and minorities tend to be affected at a much higher rate than nonminorities. Third, bacterial STDs (gonorrhea, chlamydia, bacterial vaginosis, and syphilis) can be treated and *cured* with antibiotics. Viral STDs (herpes, hepatitis, human papilloma virus [HPV], and HIV) cannot be cured. Antiviral medications can, however, be used in some of these diseases to minimize the duration of the symptoms or decrease how quickly the virus replicates itself in the body. Finally, condoms used consistently and correctly can significantly reduce transmission of those STDs that are transmitted by body fluids (gonorrhea, chlamydia, HIV, and hepatitis). By the same token, condoms may provide little or no protection for STDs that are transmitted by direct skin-to-skin contact (syphilis, HPV, and herpes).

Bacterial Sexually Transmitted Diseases

STDs caused by bacteria *can* be treated and cured by the use of antibiotics.

Gonorrhea

Known in street language as "clap," gonorrhea is caused by a bacteria called *Neisseria gonorrhoeae*. According to the CDC, gonorrhea infects over 650,000 people each year, and more than half of the reported infections in the United States involve people under twenty-five years of age.

Neisseeria gonorrhoeae is primarily sexually transmitted through body fluids such as semen, saliva, and vaginal secretions, and cannot survive outside of warm mucous membranes. A condom used correctly and consistently will minimize transmission of gonorrhea. It is not possible to contract the disease from toilet seats, towels, or drinking glasses. Primary gonorrhea (source of first detectable infection) can be transmitted orally, although instances are rare.

Symptoms: According to the Seattle King County Public Health Department, some men (10 percent) and most women (50 percent) experience no symptoms at all and sometimes not until the disease has severely damaged their reproductive organs. For some women, the disease is not detected until it has reached this advanced stage. Because the standard of care is changing and sexually active individuals are being screened for a variety of STDs with their routine exams, gonorrhea and other STDs are more likely to be detected and treated before serious complications emerge. The most common symptoms, when apparent, are

- *In men*—In the early stages, burning sensations during urination and/or cloudy discharge from the penis, epididiymitis, prostatitis, anal pain, and occasionally throat pain. In the latter stages, swelling at the base of the testicle and/or inflammation of the scrotal skin, and, rarely, arthritis.
- *In women*—In the early stages, some green or yellowish vaginal discharge and occasionally associated with pain, though this is rarely heavy. Women can also experience painful urination, rectal pain, and throat pain. In the later stages, pelvic inflammatory disease (PID), abdominal pain, and, rarely, arthritis.

Treatment: In the seventies a new mutant strain of gonorrhea bacteria emerged that is more resilient than the older strains and resistant to penicillin. It is believed that this resistant strain developed in Southeast Asia as a result of the use of black market penicillin in low doses by Vietnamese prostitutes. These low doses of penicillin killed only the weak organisms and allowed the stronger bacteria to survive and develop a resistance to penicillin. Therefore, because of increased antibiotic resistance, inadequate treatment, and poor patient compliance, penicillin is no longer the first drug of choice in treating gonorrhea. Rather, cephalosporins or fluoroquinolones are typically used to cure gonorrhea; they are significantly more expensive than penicillin. All sexual partners should be treated simultaneously to prevent reinfection. Antibiotic resistance continues to be a problem, requiring expensive and prolonged therapy. Most people respond well to treatment if the problem is diagnosed early enough, and post-treatment evaluation is often recommended to be certain the infection has been cleared. About 10 percent of cases, however, are more resistant and require extensive and costly treatment.

Complications: As mentioned earlier, 50 percent of women have no observable symptoms until the reproductive organs are significantly involved. Thus, it is common for women to spread the disease to sexual partners because they are unaware they have the disease. At least half of the women who remain untreated for two or more months are infected throughout the vagina, cervix, uterus, and fallopian tubes. The bacteria spread very quickly during menstruation, which is also the time when a woman is most likely to experience symptoms of infection. It is not until the bacteria travels out of the fallopian tubes into the abdominal cavity and onto the ovaries that noticeable pelvic symptoms occur, causing a condition known as PID. The symptoms of PID include disrupted menstrual cycles, fever, headache, vomiting, pain in the lower abdomen, and, in 20 to 30 percent of women, infertility or sterilization.

Often scar tissue forms in the fallopian tubes, partially or completely blocking the tube. When this happens, a sperm cell may bypass a partially blocked area and fertilize an ovum that consequently cannot reach the uterus through the blocked area. The result, ectopic pregnancy, is a very serious and life-threatening health hazard for the woman. The fertilized ovum must be aborted in order to protect the mother's life. If the fallopian tube is completely occluded, fertilization cannot occur and the woman is infertile.

A child born to a woman infected with gonorrhea may contract an eye infection from the birth canal. Generally, silver nitrate ointment applied at birth will prevent serious complications. A few adults have contracted gonococcal eye infection by touching their eyes immediately after handling their genitals.

Syphilis

This is a very serious STD, although less common than gonorrhea. In 1999, approximately 35,600 new cases were reported in the United States by the CDC. The numbers have steadily increased each year since. Syphilis is caused by a thin, corkscrew bacteria *(Treponema pallidum)* called a spirochete. Like the gonorrhea bacterium, the spirochete requires a warm, moist environment to survive. Syphilis is transmitted through direct skin-to-skin contact, often by sexual contact. The organism is passed from open lesions of an infected person through minor lesions of the mucosal membranes or openings in the skin of a sexual partner. The syphilis lesions are usually in the genital area but may be anywhere on the skin, such as the mouth, lips, or abdomen. A condom properly used may or may not prevent the transmission of this disease. Syphilis is one of the STDs that can result in death.

Symptoms: The disease progresses through three stages of development. (Current medical terminology refers to three stages—primary, secondary, and latent [or tertiary] syphilis. Latent and tertiary syphilis are often interchangeable, and are subdivided into early latent, late latent, and unknown duration per the CDC. The terminology is very confusing.)

Primary syphilis: Two to six weeks after exposure, a small, painless sore, or chancre, appears at the site of infection in conjunction with regional enlarged lymph nodes where the spirochete entered the body, usually in the genital area or mouth. Because the sore is small and painless, it may go unnoticed. The chancre will generally heal in one to five weeks. After it heals there are generally no symptoms of syphilis for several weeks, although the individual can still infect a sexual partner. After several weeks of remaining dormant, the disease progresses to the second stage.

Secondary syphilis: During this stage, a skin rash develops on the body, usually a few weeks (or up to six months) after the chancre appears. This rash usually does not hurt or itch. For some people the rash is rarely noticeable; for others, it is very noticeable, with hard, raised bumps.

If the individual doesn't seek treatment at this stage, the disease enters the very dangerous third stage.

Latent syphilis: Initially, during a latent, or hidden, stage of syphilis, there may be no visible symptoms for several years. The organisms, however, continue to multiply. After one year in the latent stage the individual is no longer contagious to sexual partners.

The progression of latent syphilis is extremely serious and often results in death. The symptoms may appear any time after secondary syphilis, in some cases years after the initial infection. These symptoms may include tumors of the skin, bone, lungs, and liver; blindness; paralysis; ruptured blood vessels; heart failure; and severe mental disturbances.

Treatment: The curative treatment for syphilis is penicillin, unless an individual is allergic to it, in which case tetracycline or doxycycline is given. Since there may be no symptoms evident in syphilis, an individual should have several blood tests after treatment to be sure he or she is free of the organism.

Complications: An infected pregnant woman can at any stage of the infection pass the disease on to her unborn child through the placenta, and after the first trimester of pregnancy, syphilis can cause extreme damage or death to infected babies. Therefore, it is very important for any woman with even a remote possibility of infection to be tested during the first three months of pregnancy. Latent syphilis in any individual has very severe complications.

Chlamydia Trachomatis

Caused by a one-celled bacteria, *Chlamydia trachomatis,* chlamydia is the most common and most frequently reported bacterial infection in the United States. The CDC estimates that 50 percent of sexually active women have evidence of chlamydial infection by the age of thirty.

Teenage girls, fifteen to nineteen years, have the highest rate of infection, representing 46 percent of reported infections. The CDC reports that an estimated three million cases of chlamydia are reported each year in America, with 50 percent of men and 75 percent of women having no symptoms. A woman infected with chlamydia is three to five times more likely to become infected with HIV. The chlamydia bacteria can survive outside the body for several hours in a moist environment. It is transmitted, however, through body fluids (preseminal fluid, semen, vaginal and/or rectal secretions, and saliva) during genital sexual contact. Chlamydia is not transmitted through casual contact, toilet seats, washcloths, or towels. A condom correctly and consistently used will significantly decrease or prevent the transmission of chlamydia.

Symptoms: According to the Seattle King County Public Health Department, 80 percent of women and 50 percent of men with chlamydial infection have no symptoms and are likely to transmit the infection to their sexual partners. If a woman experiences symptoms, however, she will typically describe vaginal discharge and/or painful urination, and occasionally pain in the Bartholin glands. Like gonorrhea, an infection that has advanced through the uterus to the fallopian tubes may present with PID, resulting in pelvic, abdominal, and/or back pain, nausea, fever, painful intercourse, or spotting between menstrual periods. Infection of the upper reproductive tract can, like gonorrhea, cause irreversible and permanent damage, resulting in infertility and potentially life-threatening ectopic pregnancy.

Symptomatic men will notice a discharge from the penis accompanied by painful urination. Occasionally men may also experience burning or itching at the meatus (opening of the penis) as well as an enlarged and painful prostate and swelling of the testicles. It is also possible for men to become infertile from chlamydial infection.

Treatment: Chlamydia is a bacterial infection and can be cured with an antibiotic. The most common antibiotics used to treat chlamydia are azithromycin, doxycycline, or erythromycin. As with gonorrhea, antibiotic resistance is becoming increasingly more problematic.

Complications: Frequently people infected with chlamydia are also infected with gonorrhea. Therefore, the CDC recommends that people treated for chlamydia also be treated for gonorrhea. As noted above, undiagnosed or untreated chlamydial infection may have devastating consequences, such as infertility, chronic pain, and potentially life-threatening ectopic pregnancy. These complications, not unique to chlamydial infection, are known to be closely associated with other health issues such as depression and other mental illnesses.

Bacterial Vaginosis

Bacterial vaginosis (BV) is a poorly understood but common bacterial infection in women of reproductive age caused by an imbalance of bacteria normally found in a woman's vagina. While it is considered an STD, BV may, however, develop for many reasons that are not associated with sexual activity, such as douching. Sexually active women with new or multiple partners are more likely to develop BV. BV is not transmitted from towels, toilet seats, or other casual contact. It is unclear if a condom reduces the incidence of BV infection.

Symptoms: Women with BV are typically symptomatic and will notice a white to gray, thin vaginal discharge with a foul "fishy" type odor, especially after intercourse. Women will occasionally report pain on urination, as well as external genital and/or vaginal irritation. Many women will not notice any symptoms.

Treatment: The curative treatment for BV is a medication called metronidazole (flagyl) or clindamycin. Metronidazole tends to have quite a few side effects. Male partners generally do not require treatment for BV.

Complications: Like all STDs, BV increases one's risk of acquiring other STDs. Pregnant women especially are at an increased risk of developing complications with BV infections because the bacteria causing the infection are known to precipitate premature rupture of the membranes, resulting in preterm deliveries and low birth-weight babies. It is also known that BV, like gonorrhea and chlamydia, can travel through the uterus and fallopian tubes into the pelvic cavity, causing PID or pelvic and/or abdominal pain. The fallopian tubes can be scarred and damaged by infection of the upper reproductive tract, causing infertility or ectopic pregnancy.

viral sexually transmitted diseases

STDs caused by viruses can be treated, but *cannot* be cured. In some diseases, the body's immune system may eliminate the virus, suppress the virus, or make antibodies against the virus, which may or may not render lifelong immunity against the disease.

Human Papilloma Virus

Human papilloma virus (HPV) is the virus that causes warts, including genital warts. There are over one hundred different strains, or types, of HPV, thirty of which are sexually transmitted and cause genital warts, or more seriously, subclinical infection. Subclinical infection means that there is no visible sign (genital wart). A well-researched and documented relationship exists between HPV infection and some types of cancer, particularly cervical cancer in women. Of the thirty sexually transmitted strains of HPV, four strains, numbers 16, 18, 31, and 45, are known to cause greater than 95 percent of all cases of cervical cancer. These strains are often referred to as "high-risk" HPV, tend to persist, and are difficult to treat. Visible genital warts can be treated with a variety of modalities discussed below, but subclinical infection is more common than genital warts, and no treatment is available.

Genital HPV is the most common STD. The CDC estimates that approximately twenty million people in the United States have HPV. Each year it is estimated that 5.5 million Americans are newly infected with this virus. Since, however, a significant number of people have subclinical infection, they are unaware of their infection and are transmitting it to their partners. HPV is transmitted by direct skin-to-skin contact with an infected person and, thus, a condom may not prevent transmission of the virus.

It is possible for an infant to develop HPV in the birthing process, although this is rare. If infection does occur, genital warts will usually be present in the mouth and throat of the infant.

Symptoms: In most cases of genital HPV infection there are no visible symptoms, and the infected person is not aware of the infection yet is capable of transmitting it to a sexual partner. In women, HPV infection is most often detected from an abnormal Pap smear during a routine physical exam. It is essential that all sexually active women have regular exams and Pap smears to screen for HPV infection.

Genital warts are the most common visible symptom of HPV infection and appear as soft, moist, pink or red swellings, or as flat or raised warts in the skin or on the mucous membranes. The warts will occasionally cluster and give a cauliflower type appearance. Typically genital warts will appear three to twelve weeks after infection. In some cases, however, several months or even years may elapse before a wart appears.

Treatment: Because HPV is a virus, there is no cure. Research demonstrates that some HPV infections are cleared by the body's immune system. Reactivation and reinfection with the virus is, however, common among sexually active people.

A variety of modalities can be used to treat genital warts, depending upon their size and location. Genital warts are frequently frozen with liquid nitrogen or treated chemically with podophyllum, trichloroacetic acid, or bichloroacetic acid. Patient-applied prescription medications called podofilox and imiquimod cream are also available. Most lesions require several treatments, and extensive lesions may require surgical excision.

No treatment for subclinical HPV infection is available, again stressing the importance of routine Pap smears. The high-risk strains of HPV (16, 18, 31, and 45) can cause precancerous cell changes in both men and women, which may result in cancer. The abnormal cells usually take five to ten years to develop into cancer. If the abnormal cells are detected prior to the development of cancer, they are removed surgically. Frequent and regular follow-up with a healthcare provider is necessary to screen for residual or newly developed abnormal cells. In some cases of HPV infection with high-risk strains, the body's immune system may clear the infection.

Complications: Cancer in both men and women is the most trouble-some complication of HPV infection. More than 95 percent of all cervical cancer in women is caused by HPV. Individuals infected with HPV are at a much greater risk of acquiring other STDs such as HIV. Occasionally a newborn may develop HPV infection during birth. In some instances, genital warts may enlarge during pregnancy, and some treatments may harm the developing baby in the womb.

Genital Herpes

Genital herpes is an STD caused by the herpes simplex virus (HSV). Because HSV is a virus, no cure is available. Transmission is by direct skin-to-skin contact. Thus, a condom correctly used may or may not be effective in preventing the transmission of this disease. There are two types of herpes virus. HSV type 1 is usually manifested as cold sores or blisters in the mouth, lips, or nose, and rarely in the genital area; HSV type 2 is usually manifested in the genital area and rarely in the oral area. The first outbreak with either HSV1 or HSV2 is typically the longest in duration and most painful, taking two to four weeks to clear. Subsequent outbreaks tend to be less frequent and less severe. HSV is unique in that one can unknowingly transmit the virus during periods of subclinical or asymptomatic viral shedding, which is discussed in more detail below. HSV2 will be discussed here.

HSV2: This virus currently affects sixty million people in the United States, with 500,000 to one million new cases reported each year. As noted above, herpes is spread through direct skin-to-skin sexual contact and kissing when active sores are present, and by touching active sores. The virus can survive for several hours on objects such as towels, drinking glasses, and toilet seats, but experts say that contracting herpes from those sources, although possible, is rare. It is also possible to transmit the infection, however, during subclinical and asymptomatic infection, when the infected person is shedding live, active virus, but has no signs (blisters) or symptoms (itching, pain) of infection. Asymptomatic shedding is especially problematic during childbirth. It is fortunate that neonatal herpes is rare, but is an extremely serious condition for the newborn that can result in death or permanent disabilities.

Symptoms: One or more bumps (or "papules"), clusters of blisters, or vesicles form in the genital area. They appear generally between eight and fourteen days after contact with an infected individual, although they may appear as many as twenty days after sexual exposure. These papules soon form blisters filled with a clear fluid containing the virus. This fluid is extremely infectious and may turn to pus as the body's white blood cells attack the virus. The blisters result in ulcerations of the affected area and are quite painful in most people. When the blisters rupture to form wet, painful open sores, the disease is at its most contagious stage. The sores eventually form a crust and begin to heal, which may take as long as ten days. Prior to an outbreak an itching, tingling, or burning sensation may occur where the blister will ultimately appear. These symptoms are known as the prodrome because they indicate the ultimate outbreak of blisters in the next couple of days. Prodrome symptoms can be helpful in timing of medication as well as reducing transmission of the infection.

Other common symptoms of genital herpes are swollen glands, muscle aches, fever, and pain on urination. Often the victim cannot walk or sit, and the symptoms can last four to six weeks. Some people with herpes never develop symptoms and can, as previously mentioned, unknowingly transmit the virus.

Even after blisters heal, the virus does not go away. Once an individual is infected, he or she is infected for life. The virus retreats up a spinal nerve fiber root and rests in the nerve cells adjacent to the lower spinal cord. Symptoms often recur periodically and tend to be worse in the first year after the initial outbreak as the virus returns down the fibers to the genitals, or, rarely, the oral area. Because HSV resides in dormant states in the spinal nerve root, outbreaks will always occur along the same spinal nerve, resulting in blisters in the same location. If an individual has blisters in more than one area of the body, more than one spinal nerve hosts the virus.

Treatment: At this time, no cure exists for the herpes virus. Oral antiviral medications such as acyclovir can, however, prevent or decrease the speed of virus replication, thereby limiting the severity and duration of the symptoms. For recurrent outbreaks, antiviral medication is most effective if taken during the prodrome period, if one exists. Most treatments are designed to prevent recurrent outbreaks or minimize symptoms, and to relieve pain and discomfort during an outbreak. Topical analgesic antivirals are also available that can be applied to the infected area, but oral medication is usually preferred to topical medication.

Complications: Two complications to herpes are possible in women. First, the risk of developing cancer of the cervix is five to eight times higher in women who have genital herpes than in the general population. Once an individual is infected with HSV, she or he will have it for life. Second, a newborn child is almost certain to be infected with genital herpes while passing through the birth canal. Usually, when this risk is high, a Caesarean section is performed to minimize risk to the child, but this procedure has its own set of risk factors for the mother. Almost 65 percent of infected newborns who acquire HSV during childbirth will either be severely disabled or die.

Open herpes sores are extremely contagious. The virus can spread easily and quickly to adjacent areas. It is important for both the infected individual and others to avoid touching the sores. By touching a sore and then touching another part of the body, it is possible to spread the infection. This has resulted in serious eye damage in many cases where the eyes were touched after the sores were touched. Recent studies indicate that genital herpes may be transmitted even when *no* symptoms occur during periods of asymptomatic shedding.

Human Immunodeficiency Virus (HIV) and Acquired Immune Deficiency Syndrome (AIDS)

HIV, first identified in 1983, is the virus that causes AIDS, which was identified in 1981. HIV and AIDS are not synonymous. HIV attacks and kills white blood cells known as T-cells, destroying the body's ability to fight off infection and resulting in immunodeficiency. The

CDC provides specific criteria differentiating HIV infection from AIDS. Much remains to be learned about HIV and AIDS. HIV is spread through body fluids (preseminal fluid, semen, vaginal secretions, blood, saliva, and breast milk), sexual contact, the exchange of body fluids, and by sharing intravenous (IV) needles. HIV is a very fragile virus and does not survive outside the body. It is quickly deactivated when exposed to air, soap, or disinfectants. According to the CDC, 850,000 to 900,000 Americans have HIV, many of whom are unaware of their infection. Worldwide, approximately 14,000 new infections occur per day. It takes about eight to ten years from the time an individual acquires an HIV infection until the development of AIDS.

Symptoms: Approximately 50 to 90 percent of people newly infected with HIV will describe flulike symptoms lasting two weeks to three months, while some individuals deny any symptoms. The development of AIDS as a result of HIV infection takes, in most people, between eight and ten years, as noted above. Because AIDS has a long latency period (usually five to seven years), there may be no early symptoms immediately after the disease is contracted. Following the latency period, a worsening immune system will be indicated by a broad range of AIDS symptoms, including, but not limited to, swollen lymph glands, fatigue, malaise, fever, night sweats, diarrhea, weight loss, persistent yeast infection, and Kaposi's sarcoma, an aggressive form of cancer caused by the herpes virus, as well as other types of cancer. Often, mental and neurological problems occur as the virus begins to invade the brain cells. Forgetfulness, dementia, impaired speech, tremors, and seizures gradually increase in severity.

Treatment: An arsenal of approved antiviral drugs is available for *treating* HIV infection but, at present, there is no known *cure* for HIV or AIDS. Medications do not eliminate the virus from the body, but interfere with virus replication inside the affected cells. A combination of medications is used to treat HIV because of the virus's ability to become resistant to any one drug. Extensive research is currently under way to create a vaccine for HIV, but it will be several years, if ever, before one is available because of the virus's ability to mutate. Many of the medications have drug interactions with other medications and have an extensive side-effect profile. There is no effective treatment for HIV or AIDS.

Complications: HIV infections eventually progress to AIDS, which ultimately results in death. People with HIV and AIDS are prone to a variety of illnesses due to a compromised immune system. No one has ever been known to recover from HIV or AIDS.

Viral Hepatitis

Hepatitis is an inflammation of the liver that can be caused in a variety of ways, viruses being one of them. There are several types of viral hepatitis, but hepatitis A virus (HAV or Hep. A), hepatitis B virus (HBV or Hep. B), and hepatitis C virus (HCV or Hep. C) are all known to be sexually transmitted. It is important to note, though, that a person may contract hepatitis A, B, or C in many ways that have nothing to do with sexual transmission.

Hepatitis A is transmitted by an oral-fecal route. In the context of sexual transmission, it is typically acquired through anal and oral sex. Symptoms usually occur two to six weeks after exposure, and complete recovery usually occurs in three weeks. HAV is self-limiting and the vast majority of people will make a complete recovery but do not develop lifelong immunity. A two-part vaccine series is available that can provide protection for several years.

Hepatitis B is transmitted, like HIV, through body fluids. It is also possible to transmit HBV by sharing personal hygiene products such as nail clippers and toothbrushes with an infected person. Most adults, approximately 90 percent, who acquire HBV will recover completely and develop antibodies against the infection, rendering lifelong immunity. These individuals will not transmit the infection to other people. Of the approximate 10 percent who do not recover completely, half of them will develop liver failure and likely die, and the other half will become chronic hepatitis B carriers. Chronic carriers are capable of transmitting the infection to other people even though they have no symptoms. People infected with HBV generally develop symptoms in six weeks to six months (average is two months) and most will recover in three weeks. A three-part vaccine series provides protection against HBV.

Hepatitis C is also transmitted through body fluids and the sharing of personal hygiene products and is fairly common in the IV drug user population. HCV is a fairly stable virus outside of the body and in some cases can remain active for several days or weeks. Sexual transmission is possible, but is not common. This virus typically infects an individual and remains relatively dormant in the body, often for years, before slightly elevated liver enzymes are detected in blood work. Although people infected with HCV have developed antibodies, they do recover or have lifelong immunity, and they may transmit the virus to others who come into contact with their body fluids. It is estimated by the Seattle King County Public Health Department that 3.5 million Americans have chronic HCV, and 75 to 85 percent of them become chronic carriers. As well, 80 percent of chronic carriers suffer only mild injury to their liver with minimal or no symptoms, while 10 to 20 percent develop serious liver problems twenty to thirty years after initial infection.

Symptoms: The symptoms for HAV, HBV, and HCV are similar. Most symptomatic people will describe flulike symptoms such as nausea, vomiting, loss of appetite, fever, and abdominal pain, as well as dark yellow urine and jaundice. Some people will not develop any symptoms.

Treatment: As with all viruses, there is no cure for these infections, and treatment is usually comfort measures for the symptoms. HAV is self-limiting, but it is possible to become reinfected with the virus. An immunoglobulin injection is available that, if given within a certain time frame after known exposure, will prevent the development of HAV infection. Prevention of HAV is the best treatment. Most people with HBV infection will recover and develop lifelong immunity. As with HAV, an HBV immunoglobulin is available for known exposure, and prevention is the best treatment. The treatment of HCV is complicated. As with other viral infections, antiviral medications and interferon are available, but these medications will not cure HCV. At the present time there is no vaccine available for HCV.

Complications: Most people infected with HAV or HBV suffer no long-term complications. People who become chronic carriers of HBV or have HCV are, however, capable of transmitting the infection even though they have no symptoms. Chronic HBV and HCV carriers are at an increased risk of developing chronic liver failure, cirrhosis of the liver, and liver cancer.

All of the diseases discussed in this chapter are extremely dangerous and have become national health hazards. Research will continue, discoveries will be made, and most likely new diseases will develop. But most people do have a choice as to whether they will be exposed to these diseases.

Only one solution is 100 percent effective in fighting the tremendous problem of STDs. Through that solution, most STDs, in fact, can be totally destroyed in one generation. This solution has been recognized for thousands of years, though never effectively carried out. As is true for each problem discussed in this book, the only realistic solution comes back to the clear biblical standard of marriage: one sexual partner and a lifetime commitment to remain faithful and to share that part of the relationship with no one else until the death of that partner. (Back in the "olden days" that was called morality and fidelity.) If that solution were universally practiced, STDs would be gone by the time our grandchildren were old enough to worry about them.

The road to true sexual fulfillment is full of potholes and dead-end detours. But there is a clear road map. If we follow that map, even when we'd like to take a detour that feels right at the moment, we will reach our destination.

Growing closer

If You Are Unmarried

1. What would life be like in your home if a newborn baby became a part of it? Describe that life in as much detail as possible.

2. What dreams for the future would you need to give up? What dreams would you need to modify? How?

If Your Marriage Began with a Pregnancy

1. How would your marital relationship be different had the pregnancy occurred after the wedding?
2. What *specifically* is keeping your marriage from developing these positive aspects now?
3. Do you need to forgive someone in order to make these adjustments? Do you need to forgive yourself?
4. Read John 8:1–11. Make some decisions regarding how you will respond to past poor decisions, both your own and those of others.

Endnotes

chapter 1: uncovering the trap

1. *U.S. News and World Report*, 19 May 1997, 54–59.
2. Guttmacher Institute, *Sex and America's Teenagers* (New York: Guttmacher Institute, 1994), 38.
3. P. Donovan, *Testing Positive: Sexually Transmitted Disease and the Public Health Response* (New York: AGI, 1993), 24.
4. Guttmacher Institute, *Teenage Pregnancy: Overall Trends and State-by-state Information* (New York: Guttmacher Institute, 1999).
5. Ibid.
6. Guttmacher Institute, *Sex and America's Teenagers*, 19–20.

chapter 3: cohabitation confusion

1. David Popenoe and Barbara Defoe Whitehead, "Should We Live Together? What Young Adults Need to Know About Cohabitation Before Marriage," *The National Marriage Project*, January 1999, 3–4.
2. Alfred DeMaris and K. Vaninadjha Rao, "Premarital Cohabitation and Subsequent Marital Stability in the United States: A Reassessment," *Journal of Marriage and Family* 54 (1992): 178–90.
3. "Cohabitation Crisis," *Nebraska Citizen* 5, no. 3 (March 2002).
4. Jan E. Stets, "The Link Between Past and Present Intimate Relationships," *Journal of Family Issues* 14 (1993): 236–60.

5. Sonia Miner Salari and Bret M. Baldwin, "Verbal, Physical and Injurious Aggression Among Intimate Couples over Time," *Journal of Family Issues* 23 (May 2000): 523–50.

6. Bureau of Justice Statistics, *Intimate Partner Violence* (The National Crime Victimization Survey, U.S. Department of Justice, Washington D.C., May 2000), 4–5.

7. Allan V. Horowitz et al., "The Relationship Between Cohabitation and Mental Health: A Study of Young Adult Cohorts," *Journal of Marriage and the Family* 60 (1998): 505–14.

8. Popenoe and Whitehead, "Should We Live Together?" 7.

9. Susan L. Brown, "Child Well-Being in Cohabiting Families," in *Just Living Together: Implications of Cohabitation on Families, Children and Social Policy,* ed. Alan Booth and Ann C. Crouter (Mahwah, N.J.: Lawrence Erlbaum Assoc., 2002), 173–87.

10. Popenoe and Whitehead, "Should We Live Together?" 8.

11. Robert Whelon, *Broken Homes and Battered Children: A Study of the Relationship Between Child Abuse and Family Type* (London, England: Family Education Trust, 1993), 29.

12. Robert Schoen and Robin M. Weinick, "Partner Choice in Marriages and Cohabitations," *Journal of Marriage and the Family* 55 (1993): 408–14.

13. Susan L. Brown and Alan Both, "Cohabitation Versus Marriage: A Comparison of Relationship Quality," *Journal of Marriage and the Family* 58 (1996): 668–78.

14. Barbara Foley Wilson and Sally Cunningham Clark, "Remarriages: A Demographic Profile," *Journal of Family Issues* 13 (1992): 123–41.

15. U.S. Census Bureau, "Unmarried Couple Households, by Presence of Children: 1960 to Present" (Washington, D.C.: U.S. Census Bureau, 29 June 2001), table UC-1.

16. "Monitoring the Future Survey" (Survey Research Center, University of Michigan, 1995). Quoted in Popenoe and Whitehead, "Should We Live Together?" 3.

17. Judith Treas and Deirdre Giesen, "Sexual Infidelity Among Married and Cohabiting Americans," *Journal of Marriage and the Family* 62 (2000): 48–60.

18. National Marriage Project, *The State of Our Unions 2000: The Social Health of Marriage in America* (New Brunswick, N.J.: The National Marriage Project, 2000).

19. Paul R. Amato and Alan Booth, *A Generation at Risk* (Cambridge, Mass.: Harvard University Press, 1997), 258, table 4-2.

20. Linda J. Waite and Maggie Gallagher, *The Case for Marriage: Why Married People Are Happier, Healthier and Better-off Financially* (New York: Doubleday, 2000).

chapter 4: The Illicit Effect

1. Helen Singer Kaplan, *The New Sex Therapy* (New York: Brunner/Mazel, 1974), 159.

2. Donald Joy, *Re-Bonding: Preventing and Restoring Damaged Relationships* (Nappanee, Ind.: Evangel Publishing House, 2000).

3. Ed Wheat and Gaye Wheat, *Intended for Pleasure,* 3d rev. ed. (Grand Rapids: Revell, 1997).

chapter 5: The Technical Virginity Trap

1. Desmond Morris, *Intimate Behavior* (New York: Random House, 1971), 74–78.

2. Tim Stafford, "Love, Sex and the Whole Person," *Campus Life,* December 1987, 8. Used by permission.

3. Michael R. Crosby, *Sex in the Bible: An Introduction to What the Scriptures Teach Us About Sexuality* (Upper Saddle River, N.J.: Prentice-Hall, 1984), 172, 176.

chapter 6: Sexual Addiction

1. Patrick Carnes, *Out of the Shadows* (Minneapolis: CompCare Publishers, 1983), 4.

2. Ibid., 10.

3. Sexaholics Anonymous, copyright © 1985 by S.A. Literature. Reprinted by permission.

4. Claire W., *God, Help Me Stop* (P.O. Box 27364, San Diego, Calif., 1982).

5. Grateful Members, *The Twelve Steps for Everyone* (Minneapolis, Minn.: CompCare Publications, 1975).

6. Sexaholics Anonymous, copyright © 1985 by S.A. Literature. Reprinted by permission.

Chapter 7: The other side of the coin

1. Joseph Dillow, *Solomon on Sex* (Nashville: Thomas Nelson, 1982), 24.
2. David Hocking, *Romantic Lovers* (Eugene, Ore.: Harvest House, 1987).
3. Dillow, *Solomon on Sex*.

Chapter 8: Discovering freedom

1. Dwight Carlson, *Sex and the Single Christian* (Ventura, Calif.: Regal Books, 1985), 53.

Chapter 9: A very, very old message

1. Joseph Dillow, *Solomon on Sex* (Nashville: Thomas Nelson, 1982), 24.

Appendix: "Hello, Doctor . . . ?"

1. U.S. Teenage Pregnancy Statistics, Allan Guttmacher Institute, March 5, 2001.
2. Sara Mclanahan and Gary Sandefur, *Growing Up With a Single Parent: What Hurts, What Helps* (Cambridge: Harvard University Press, 1994), 2.
3. Pat Fagan, "How Broken Families Rob Children of Their Chances for Prosperity," *Heritage Backgrounder* no. 1283 (June 11, 1999), 14.
4. Anne Speckhard, cited in Josh McDowell, *Why Wait? What You Need to Know About the Teen Sexuality Crisis* (San Bernardino, Calif.: Here's Life, 1987), 218.
5. Ed Wheat and Gaye Wheat, *Intended for Pleasure*, 3d rev. ed. (Grand Rapids: Revell, 1997).